teams

brilliant

teams

second edition

What to know, do and say to make a brilliant team

Douglas Miller

Prentice Hall
is an imprint of

Harlow, England • London • New York • Boston • San Francisco • Toronto • Sydney • Singapore • Hong Kong
Tokyo • Seoul • Taipei • New Delhi • Cape Town • Madrid • Mexico City • Amsterdam • Munich • Paris • Milan

PEARSON EDUCATION LIMITED

Edinburgh Gate
Harlow CM20 2JE
Tel: +44 (0)1279 623623
Fax: +44 (0)1279 431059
Website: www.pearsoned.co.uk

First published in Great Britain in 2008
Second edition published 2011

© Pearson Education 2008, 2011

The right of Douglas Miller to be identified as author of this work has been asserted by him in accordance with the Copyright, Designs and Patents Act 1988.

Pearson Education is not responsible for the content of third party internet sites.

ISBN: 978-0-273-74474-0

British Library Cataloguing-in-Publication Data
A catalogue record for this book is available from the British Library

Library of Congress Cataloging-in-Publication Data
Miller, Douglas, 1966-
  Brilliant teams : what to know, do and say to make a brilliant team / Douglas Miller. -- 2nd ed.
    p.cm.
  Includes bibliographical references.
  ISBN 978-0-273-74474-0 (pbk.)
  1. Teams in the workplace. I. Title.
  HD66.M5445 2011
  658.4'022--dc22
                                          2010050448

The publishers would like to thank Mark Brown for permission to reproduce Figure 5.1 from Brown, M (1993) *The Dinosaur Strain*, ICE Books.

10 9 8 7 6 5 4 3 2 1
15 14 13 12 11

Typeset in 10/14pt Plantin by 30
Printed and bound in Great Britain by Henry Ling Ltd, at The Dorset Press, Dorchester, Dorset

Contents

About the author   vi
Acknowledgements   vii
Introduction   viii

part 1 How to be a brilliant team   1

1   It starts with YOU   3
2   You and your team relationships   19
3   What's in a brilliant team?   49
4   Teams and leadership   69
5   Setting team goals   87
6   Team meetings and briefings   107
7   Teams and decision making   123
8   Teams under pressure   141
9   The 10 classic team traps   151

part 2 Brilliant team types   165

10 Creative and problem-solving teams   167
11 Project teams   185
12 Remote teams   201

Conclusion   213
References and acknowledgements   215

About the author

Douglas Miller is a successful writer, speaker and trainer. He runs lively team-building events and retreats in many countries around the world for groups of 10–200 people. As a trainer and speaker he works regularly for the United Nations and its different agencies, the Organisation for Security and Co-operation in Europe and the European Central Bank, as well as for many private sector organisations.

Brilliant Teams is his sixth book.

Further information on Douglas can be found at **www.douglasmillerlearning.com**.

Acknowledgements

I would like to thank the following:

- Alan Chapman at businessballs.com for his continuing support and encouragement.
- Mark Brown at Innovation Centre Europe for the many observations and inspirational thoughts that he has allowed me to use in this and other books.
- Arlind Bakraci and his team whose ongoing support has allowed me to 'air' so much of my learning material.

Finally I would like to thank Sam Jackson, my Commissioning Editor at Pearson, for her patience, flexibility and sound advice, Caroline Jordan for her persistence and responsiveness, and Emma Devlin, Linda Dhondy, Jill Birch and Nikki Tomlinson for making the book readable. Any errors and oversights are my responsibility.

Introduction

We have two hands. One is for helping ourselves and the other is for helping others.   Audrey Hepburn

Any organisation – a business, a not-for-profit 'enterprise', a sports team or a club – depends on great teamwork for its success. It is at that moment – the moment of 'success' – when we can truly say we were, or are, a 'brilliant' team. This book shows how you generate high-performance, results-focused, successful teams no matter what environment you operate in. Not only does it show how to grow brilliant teams but how you can play your part.

The word 'team' is often misused. When people use the word 'team' what they really mean is a collection of individuals or a working group or party. Think of the sports team near to relegation, underperforming and less than the sum of its individual parts. The manager announces the 'team' for the next game. What the manager is actually announcing is a group of individuals who he or she hopes might become a team.

You are probably working in a team of some kind right now. But are you really a team? Is there something missing? Do you have a gut feeling that you could achieve more but are not sure how? Are you just 'treading water' rather than stretching out? If you feel any or all of these things apply to you and your group, and you want your group to become a great team, then this book can help you.

This is a book that will help you and your team be better regardless of whether you lead the team or are a team member.

The aspiration – being a brilliant team

So, who *doesn't* work in a team? Teams are the beating heart of any successful organisation and everyone who works in them. But teams, like people, come in many different shapes and forms and make differing demands on the people that work in them. The nature of the work that the team undertakes will affect the way in which individuals in those teams need to operate. However, there are 10 universal factors that apply to almost any team in any situation and which, if they are followed, can help you become a brilliant team.

> there are 10 universal factors that apply to almost any team

Your team will become brilliant when you:

1 Commit to a shared, agreed goal – the desired 'result'.

2 Are clear what the team has to do to achieve the 'result'.

3 Have a shared desire to overcome problems and challenges.

4 Understand how the team relates to the world beyond.

5 Maximise opportunities.

6 Create a culture of mutually beneficial feedback – so that performance standards get systematically raised.

7 Learn and develop as a team – so that performance standards get raised.

8 Achieve more as an individual than you could if you were acting alone.

9 Get the 'results' the team desires.

10 Don't sit back when the team achieves its goals – the team moves on to the next goal.

If you aspire to be part of a brilliant team then these 10 factors will help you to do so. This book will help you and your team colleagues to meet your collective aspiration.

Why be part of a brilliant team?

Imagine that you decide to look for another job. You trawl through the internet, newspapers and magazines for ads that interest you. You notice one thing that is common to all of them. The phrases 'good team worker' or 'good team player' are the common currency of nearly all job advertisements. But while a prospective employer wants great team workers, nearly all of us rightly ask the *'What's in it for me?'* question. In fact there is a lot 'in it for you'. Being part of a brilliant team has fantastic benefits for you personally:

- Brilliant teams are successful teams – they deliver results. Being associated with success is so much more exciting than failure or mediocrity.
- Brilliant teams form the bedrock of any successful organisation. Without brilliant teams the organisation rapidly becomes far less than the sum of its parts and a soul-destroying place to work. Sadly many people accept this as a reality of working life for many years when it doesn't need to be that way at all.
- Brilliant teams help you as a team member to develop and grow as a person and a performer.
- Brilliant teams help you to do so much more than you ever could alone.
- Brilliant teams maximise the potential of all individuals – including you.
- Brilliant teams can provide the essential energy and support for your own ideas.

● Brilliant teams make the working day fly by. Bad working atmospheres create long, depressing days. Great team environments create fast-moving, fun, productive places to work. Being part of a brilliant team opens up the possibility that you might just look forward to the alarm clock going off in the morning.

How is this book structured?

This book comes in two parts. Part 1: How to be a brilliant team examines the universal factors involved in building a brilliant team such as team composition, team leadership, generating goals and having dynamic, productive meetings.

In many places in this book the emphasis is firmly on you, the team member, and the part you can play in building a brilliant team. What are the personal qualities and approaches required from individual team members to make teams succeed? Chapter 1: It starts with YOU is the starting point for the answers to this question. However, the book will often also talk to you collectively as a team and how you can collaborate to create a great team. Chapter 5: Setting team goals is a good example of this.

While all brilliant teams share some universal characteristics that take them from not so good to good to great, there are also certain characteristics that will propel specialist teams in this same positive direction. First, all organisations have various kinds of specialist teams operating within them. Second, every team has to be adaptable: at different times your team at work or in your leisure pursuit may have to be creative, take a project-based approach or adapt when the team is dispersed. You may

> every team has to be adaptable

need to be all of these things at the same time. So at different times your own team will need to be adaptable in its working practices and as team players you, as individuals, need to show flexibility of approach.

Part 2: Brilliant team types offers advice for teams doing particular kinds of work across three shorter chapters:

- Chapter 10: Creative and problem-solving teams – where a more creative approach is required from a team to drive the organisation forward or to solve particular, perhaps long-standing, problems.
- Chapter 11: Project teams – where a team is working on a specific 'one-off' piece of work.
- Chapter 12: Remote teams – where the team and team members are located away from the central 'hub'. Sales teams and teams operating internationally are such examples.

Team working 'zeitgeist'

Studies about what makes great teams, alongside technological advances, are changing the ways teams operate. These changes have influenced the 'tone' of this book. The book acknowledges that team members are increasingly empowered to take the initiative, make decisions and communicate vertically and horizontally without going through approved channels. Over the past 10–15 years the following trends have become clear:

- Technological advances are changing communication methods in the team. Both in America and Europe, for example, social networking is increasingly used as a way to problem solve among team members. Traditionally those team members may have gone to their manager or team leader for advice. Now they bypass the leader.
- The 'net gen' (born after 1977) communicate in ways that more senior managers may not understand. This means that this group – and you may be one of them – have to 'self-organise' to get the job done.

- It's recognised that we respond best to team goals when we have input into their setting. This has been the case for many years but it has taken time for senior management to learn the benefits of 'letting go'.

- The breaking down of organisational hierarchies has meant that teams can make decisions quicker and therefore act faster.

- Teams are often 'self-managed' – less likely to be reporting upwards through a rigid hierarchical structure. They have a greater degree of autonomy than ever before.

- Even if team members work at different levels in an organisation they will often meet as equals. Everyone's views and opinions are lent equal weight.

While some of you may not recognise this in your own team – *'Who are you trying to kid Doug!'* – many of you will at least be moving in these directions if you look at where you were say 10 years ago. Chapter 12: Remote teams is the last chapter of this book and is designed to help you if you are working in teams that are adopting these twenty-first century approaches.

Great people = Great team?

It happens a lot in music and sport. In the 1970s great individual rock musicians came together to form 'supergroups' but the end result was self-indulgent, bloated and formulaic music. In sports such as football (global version) we see managers being thrown lots of money by indulgent club owners and signing great players but the end result is frequently not the desired one. There are, of course, many exceptions to this. And it works the other way too. Plenty of sports teams with few outstanding players have performed beyond the level of the individual talents of the team, as though one plus one can make three. And in music too we see moderate musicians combining to produce a stellar sound.

So, do we create a brilliant team by bringing the best people together? There is plenty of evidence to suggest it is not quite as simple as that. The best may mean the brightest, the most naturally talented and/or those that have met with great success in the past. But somehow 'the best' come together and seem not to match up to or exceed the sum of the parts. It's a bit like baking a cake where the best ingredients are assembled and yet the end product seems flat and uninspiring.

Your team leader (perhaps that person is you) has a responsibility to get the best out of the team, but in the modern world we have moved a long way from this responsibility being in the hands of one person. That is why the first section of the first chapter of this book doesn't look at team working at all but at the attitude and energy you personally bring to the team. A brilliant team starts with *you*.

your team leader has a responsibility to get the best out of the team

PART 1

How to be a brilliant team

CHAPTER 1

It starts with YOU

Everybody has inner doubts. You've got to realise that. But what can they do to you? ... I want to play. I want to have fun. And you've got to realise that those great moments, when you're playing, when it's almost like self-hypnosis, when you're almost outside your body watching yourself play and when everything you play turns to gold; nothing goes wrong; the group is swinging and you can do anything you want, even things you thought you could never do.

Shelley Manne, jazz musician

S helley Manne describes beautifully the feeling you get when you are completely lost in what you are doing. How great to be absorbed, consumed, stimulated, immersed in a group activity. All recognisable feelings to those who have experienced what has been called the state of 'flow'. And what a great justification for being part of a team – *doing things you thought you could never do.* Jazz music is a great metaphor here because it is based around wonderful rhythm and interconnectivity between group/team members. Those who have been in this state of 'flow' – at work or leisure – will recognise the perfect sense of rhythm and synchronicity they feel when they go about what they are doing. It gives you one of those perfect 'life is really worth living' feelings. The team and individuals perform in superb harmony and achieve beyond a level some – including they – may have thought possible. The key with this team state is that it is wonderfully productive.

But these wonderful feelings and great productivity do not happen by themselves. They begin with you and the attitude you have to the team and its activities.

Musicians are dedicated and a degree of singular thinking is required to become a great musician. But the saxophone player, for instance, knows that the saxophone solo is meaningless without great support from the rest of band. The rhythm created by the percussion and the bass guitar have to be 'tight' to show the saxophonist in their best light. Even in the most egocentric of environments team support is essential. This works both ways: How can you support other team members better? What support do you need?

> even in the most egocentric of environments team support is essential

In this first chapter we look at where the team starts – the individuals in it – and in particular the attitude and energy you bring to the team. It's about your personal accountability to the team.

Personal accountability

Personal accountability begins with two key ingredients:

1   Positive attitude.
2   Positive energy.

In brilliant team working you are accountable to your team mates for any drop in attitude or energy as you help the team set about achieving its goals. There are, of course, many other attributes that brilliant teams require but these two factors are where it all begins. Without these any group of people will find it hard to gel into a brilliant team and maximise the possibilities on offer.

Accountability and the 100 club

Here is an illustration of what it means if you fall short in your attitude to the team's work and the energy you put into it. It's an impact measurement tool for you to use and it works in four steps.

Step one

Give a value of 10 out of a possible score of 10 when you give the maximum *energy* you are capable of giving to the team's work.

Step two

Imagine that you also apply the same '10 out of 10' principle when you give out the best *attitude* to team members and in the way you approach the team's work.

Step three

Multiply the two 10s together and you get the perfect 100 score (assuming you have scored 10 in each dimension) and have gained membership to the 100 club.

This final 'score' is an indication of the impact you have measured against the impact you are *capable* of achieving. In this case 100 per cent.

Step four

Now think about the work of your team. Pick a recent piece of the team's work that you were involved in and give a score out of 10 related to the energy and attitude you applied to that work. Then multiply them together. That score is your impact relative to the impact you are capable of achieving.

What is interesting is how quickly your overall percentage score drops when you drop only one or two points in either dimension:

	Positive attitude ×	Positive energy =	Percentage total (as a percentage of the impact you are capable of having)
Score	9	10	90
Score	10	9	90
Score	9	9	81
Score	9	8	72
Score	8	9	72

You can see that just a small drop in your own standards leads to an exponential drop in the positive impact you can have on the team and the work it does. Giving half of what you are capable of in both dimensions (scoring a 5 on each) does not lead to a 50 per cent impact: it leads to a 25 per cent impact (5 × 5). At this level you really are of little use to the team. These scores are of course subjective and that subjectivity needs to be infused with a huge dose of honesty.

It is not about what you give *vis-à-vis* each other in the team – this is not a competitive sport like the scoring of the perfect 10 we see in some sports at the Olympic Games. This is about what you give relative to what you are *capable* of giving. Everyone has different intrinsic attitude and energy levels.

none of us are born 'inert'

Some of us have to work a bit or a lot harder to maximise our attitude and energy potential. But none of us are born 'inert'. We are all born 'ert'. That is to say we are all born with character traits that dispose us to be, to a greater or lesser extent, 'positive'.

Who's going to notice when you are less than 'brilliant'?

Do you have days when you don't really feel like giving your all? You've had a late night the night before or have woken up in the morning feeling a bit disconnected (or both). So you might say, 'Who's going to notice if I am operating at less than my best?'

Well, once or twice might make little difference to your colleagues – although it might make a huge difference if you are in front of customers – but once you know you can get away with the drop then it starts to become a habit. In fact you may not even notice your own standards dropping, but your colleagues do. And they quickly move into one of two camps:

1 One group of team mates will see the drop in standard as 'the new standard' and their standard will drop accordingly.

Or

2 The other group – the less impressionable – will develop a lower opinion of you and what you are capable of. You become a 'space-filler' within a reduced performance environment rather than a 'collaborator' in a brilliantly effective team.

brilliant example

Here's a good illustration of how beneficial a positive attitude can be. Have you ever thought how many hours you might spend at work in your lifetime? The answer – probably between 80,000 and 100,000 hours. To those with a poor attitude that might be a depressing statistic. It's an awfully long time to be bored, unchallenged and disengaged from the team and its work. Those with a great attitude will recognise too that this is a long time. But the difference is that they will resolve to make the most of it. They will give their best to the team's work, to the challenges that the team will meet and to team colleagues. And they will look back on all those hours as time well spent – full of effort, fulfilment and fun. It's your choice. What would you like to say about how you spent your time at work when it comes to an end?

Energy and attitude

The Deva Partnership have used energy and attitude in an interesting way to illustrate the different kinds of characteristics we take on in the service of others – in our case team collaborators. They developed the energy investment model from work done by a group of consultants (see the References and acknowledgements section for more on this) to illustrate what happens when we combine attitude and energy to best effect – and of course what happens when we offer little of either. I have further adapted their model.

The energy investment model (see Figure 1.1) has 'attitude' on its vertical axis – the better the attitude you present to colleagues the higher up the axis you move. The same principle applies to the horizontal axis where 'energy' is the measure.

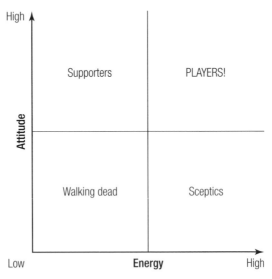

Figure 1.1 The energy investment model

You can make the assumption that the low attitude/low energy types – the walking dead – are not what brilliant teams require. But beyond that it is not quite so simple as to say teams need 100 per cent players in all teams.

Being a 'playing' supporter

Supporters may often be watchers rather than active participants in group activity – hence the name 'supporters'. The supporters, for example, are often the thinkers in the team but they may well not be inclined to proffer their views and perspectives. Shyness, fear of being put down or a sense that what they say may not have value may stop the quieter supporters from saying what they think. And what the supporters think may well be invaluable. But it might be just that thinking and action (action being the behaviour most associated with players) do not always happily coexist in the same person.

There is, however, no reason why supporters cannot be 'playing' supporters. Take a look at the 'playing' supporter version of the energy investment model in Figure 1.2 and you can see that the supporter quadrant has been sub-divided to give the supporter the option of choosing to play more – the point marked with an X. You may not feel comfortable leaping into the final quadrant (often on the basis, rightly, that it is hard to 'do' and to 'think' at the same time).

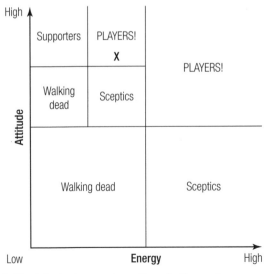

Figure 1.2 The 'playing' supporter – X marks the spot

Supporters who want to 'play' more

Step by step

Just as a small drop in attitude or energy leads to a big drop in overall impact (as you saw in the '100 club' model) so even a small increase in either dimension will lead to an exponential increase in impact. If you are currently a low-scoring performer you might find it difficult to jump right up to 9 or 10 in each dimension. But small incremental steps will make a significant difference to your performance and the performance of the team.

You are valuable

Although supporters are not necessarily life's initiators, preferring to 'support'/follow the 'players', have the confidence to believe that your thoughts, ideas and suggestions have value. A word here too for those who aren't supporters. Value the contribution non-playing team members can make – even when they are not in the front line. For example, although not everyone can 'play', every great sports team has a huge backroom staff that form an essential element in the success or failure of that team. They 'play' their part even if they are not actually playing.

> value the contribution non-playing team members can make

Value your role

Remember that being a supporter does not mean no contribution. Imagine a play or a football match with no audience or crowd at all. The audience is an integral part of the right 'mix'.

Thoughts into action

Supporters are often thinkers. But thoughts in themselves are meaningless. It is only when the thought is shared and then, if agreed, combined with action that your original thought has any value to the team.

A sceptic with positive attitude

Perhaps you have seen it all before? Perhaps you are unsure about the direction the team's heading? Maybe you are concerned that with all the change going on you are throwing away all of the best bits about what you do too? Perhaps you don't think that the team has thought things through properly? If you hold these views you may well be justified in having them. Too often teams jump into the future without really thinking through the consequences of actions or of counter-evidence. In this situation the 'sceptic' can play an important role, but it is a role that sceptics can abuse. There are two ways to approach this from the sceptic's point of view:

1 They can be a sceptic that chooses to be a 'player', i.e. to use their scepticism for positive ends.

Or

2 They can be the sceptic that joins the 'walking dead' group – going round spreading apathy and inertia wherever they go and adding to the list of walking dead within the team. The sceptics are often the people who 'yes...but' – as in '*yes* it's a good idea *but* we can't do it because...'. This approach is not usually helpful.

Just like the supporters, the sceptics can sub-divide their quadrant into four sub-quadrants as we see in Figure 1.3 overleaf.

Many of the protestations of negative sceptics become self-fulfilling prophecies. Saying 'it won't work' and then doing nothing because you hold this view will, of course, create the exact circumstances you envisaged given that action is required by the team to make anything work. And if 'it' didn't work, was it because you and a few like-minded individuals made sure it didn't through your own inaction?

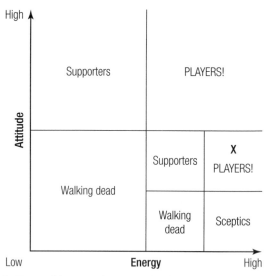

Figure 1.3 The positive sceptic – X marks the spot

Let's be clear that we are not talking about blind faith in championing an idea, suggestion or action that comes from another team member. Sceptics have great value in the team because they provide the essential level-headedness that teams need.

brilliant dos and don'ts

Do

✔ Use your scepticism for positive ends. Don't use it as a means to stop everything the team does but as a means to make sure that the actions the team takes are considered and thought through.

✔ Think about the language you use with team collaborators. For example, language that is always critical and never encouraging or which suggests, without due thought, ways in which ideas will not work kills off the energy of the team.

✔ Consider the consequences of your actions if you have a tendency to think negatively. How does it affect the team?

brilliant tip

Teams consisting entirely of players might be crazy places. Teams
need balance – as we shall see in the next chapter on team roles.
The sceptics and supporters have a part to play too. If you are
inclined to scepticism or to sit back and think while others jump into
action you should not see yourself as 'inferior' in any way. Inferiority
only comes when we fail to contribute at all to the team or when
our contribution is a deliberately destructive one.

Brilliant teams that win – getting into team 'flow'

Teams that get in the 'flow' do so when they are able to channel great attitude and energy into a unifying purpose (the goal
or 'vision' that the team has) that transcends all of the other
things that team members could be doing. That unifying sense
of purpose is reflected in the behaviours that we display as team
members when we go about the team's work and in the way the
team operates as a unit.

You will not be in flow all the time – or indeed for the majority of
the time. But the more often the team moves to the flow state the
more successful it will be. A team cannot just turn on the flow
state at will. However, there are some common characteristics
shared by teams in flow and by the people in the team.

From a team perspective:

- When the team is absolutely clear about its direction (see
  Chapter 5 on vision and goals) then the team knows what
  it is trying to achieve and every team member is clear about
  how they play their part. In this context both team and team
  members feel a degree of pressure to achieve but are not
  suffering team or personal stress as they strive to do so.

- The team has a culture of positive feedback, praise and encouragement (see Chapter 2 on relationships).
- Individual team members do not have to get on personally. They value the knowledge and skills that each team member brings to the team regardless of friendship status.
- A climate of trust exists between team members.
- The team often operates in near silence because team members are transfixed by the work they are doing; or the team operates at high volume because of the need for continuous communication between team members – a sports team in action, for example.

Sometimes things happen that cannot be planned for. The 'flow' team doesn't indulge in argument, recrimination and blame. Instead it gets on with solving the problem or meeting the challenge. Mistakes, problems and challenges should bring the team together in a collective desire to learn from mistakes, problem solve and both respond to and enjoy the challenges ahead.

From a team member's perspective:

- Team members don't point accusatory fingers at other team members when things go wrong. They look at what they can do better next time. They self-reflect first when things don't go as planned.
- Each team member, when their specialist skills and knowledge are called upon, is able to perform a leadership role.
- When other team members need help you are there. You are not afraid to ask for help either.
- Time passes by quickly. When you are lost in what you are doing you lose all sense of time. Clock watching does not occur to you or the team as a whole.
- You perform for your team mates. Teams are the best manifestation of what it is to be a social human being – the one that works with and for others.

⏵ brilliant example

England rugby manager and world-cup winning captain Martin Johnson once said that when it came to crunch time it wasn't about who you were playing for – your club or your country – but about who you were playing with. For him, his team mates mattered the most. Before he went out on the pitch he looked around the changing room and realised he was doing it for them. He did not want to let them down.

Is it too fanciful to expect us to think like this at work or in our leisure time when we are part of a group of people setting out to achieve something?

'Flow' teams have motivated people. Motivation is not a tap you can switch on all of the time but you can do little things to motivate yourself a bit more – particularly with some of the things you may not be so keen on doing. With the less exciting tasks, you and team mates can set mini-targets –

> 'flow' teams have motivated people

'by 11am we will have done this', for example – as a way of getting the less interesting stuff done and out of the way.

⏵ brilliant example

This first chapter ends where it began – with music. Watch a great group of musicians and see how they interact with each other. First, observe how they seem 'lost' in what they are doing – a true state of 'flow'. But also observe how each is aware of their individual role within the jazz band, rock group or orchestra.

Observe a great jazz band and see the way each band member looks at the other musicians, taking their cues from each other through a nod of the head perhaps – the smallest signal sends the players off into another dimension. Sometimes they seem to be operating on a purely instinctive level – something that can really only occur when you have absolute faith and trust in your fellow band members. Where mistakes are made – and they often are – then other players can take over and the listener doesn't realise. They have a great sense of how they connect with each other – what they are playing musically only has meaning when placed in the wider context of the overall group and what they are playing too. What is critical is that each person is able to express their individuality and deliver for the team at the same time.

brilliant recap

You may not notice a drop in your standards when you 'don't quite feel like it'. But everyone else does – team members, colleagues and, critically, external customers too. It can be hard to do but team collaborators rely on you to keep yourself 'up'.

We are all different. But like often attracts like. The players are attracted to the players, and so on, and perhaps value their contribution most. Whether a player, a spectator or a sceptic, each has a role to be equally valued.

Recognise the critical role you personally play in creating team 'flow'.

This chapter makes it clear that teams are only as good as the attitudes of the people in the team. Only then does it make sense to look at the tools available to help turn a great, 'tuned-in' group of people into a world-class, high-performing team. The following chapters look at how you can do this, starting by developing the strongest relationships possible between team members.

CHAPTER 2

You and your team relationships

Many people with IQs of 160 work for people with IQs of 100, if the former have poor intrapersonal intelligence and the latter have a high one. And in the day-to-day world no intelligence is more important than the interpersonal. If you don't have it you'll make poor choices about who to marry, what job to take and so on.

Multiple Intelligence pioneer Howard Gardner quoted in
Emotional Intelligence by Daniel Goleman

Your attitude to your team mates

The last chapter explored your attitude to the team's work as a whole and to the work you do as an individual for the team. This chapter looks at you and your attitude to your colleagues in the team. It looks at how you can build strong, mutually productive relationships that will benefit the team. This comprises the first section of the chapter and ends with a 'brilliant recap'. The second section shows how positive relationships can help your team learn together so that it can deal with current problems more effectively, as well as helping it to create a wider knowledge base for the future. This section also ends with a brilliant recap.

You are unlikely to be able to choose team colleagues but you can choose your attitude to them – the attitude is likely to deliver the best results for the team as a whole.

It actually comes down to this. You aren't paid to work – you are paid to get results. But you cannot hope to get the result unless you are prepared to adopt collaborative, participative, people-centred approaches with a wider circle of people – the people you operate most closely with. In other words you are extremely unlikely to get the result unless you can shape yourself into a successful team worker.

> you aren't paid to work – you are paid to get results

But the result doesn't come from solitary activity. Results come from you expressing the best things about yourself in your working environment as part of a larger group of people – your team. See yourself as a collaborator: somebody working *with* one or more people to *achieve* something.

brilliant tip

The value of relationships

If the branches of a tree mirror your team's performance then the roots of that tree are your team's relationships. The stronger the roots, the richer and more abundant will be its branches. If you want to be part of a strong team then feed and nurture the roots.

The 3 Rs – governing principles

All great teams start from a solid base. Just as in life where the 3 Rs – rules, rights and respect – form part of a good education, these 3 Rs also provide a firm basis for developing strong interpersonal relationships in the team.

Rules

Teams should establish a set of ground rules based around behavioural norms that the team can agree to. Some of these may be unique to the work you do, others are universal modes of behaviour. These are particularly important when teams are newly formed or where conflict, negativity and poor relationships are pervasive in the team. These ground rules might include:

- One in, all in – we work together to solve team problems.
- Open and honest communication.
- Criticism being based on tasks, processes and ideas and not directed at people.
- Acknowledging the rights of all team members (see Rights below).
- Respect for each other (see Respect below).
- Constructive debate rather than destructive 'finger pointing'.
- It not being about who you are – it is what you bring to the team that counts.

Rights

Everyone has rights at work, or indeed in life, including you. Think about what your rights are for the moment. Some of them might include:

- The right to be listened to.
- The right not to be discriminated against because of gender, age, race, physical ability/disability, sexual orientation or the colour of your skin.
- The right to say 'no'.
- The right to disagree.
- The right to say what you think.
- The right to be respected (see Respect below).

Just as you have rights – and do add to this list if you wish – so others in the team have rights too. In other words, whatever rights you believe you have – and just remember how frustrating it can be when you don't get listened to or when your objections get ignored – you must extend those self-same rights to others. These will be reflected in your behaviour to team colleagues.

Respect

brilliant example

An old parable

The scene: An uncle sat at the roadside in nineteenth-century Ireland with his nephew. A traveller walked by.

'Good day sir,' he said, 'I am travelling to the village over the hill. Can you tell me what the people are like there?' 'Well,' said the uncle, 'you've just been to the village on this side of the hill, how did you find the people there?' 'Oh, they were great,' said the traveller, 'really friendly, really welcoming.'

'Well, that's good to hear,' said the uncle, 'because that's just what the people are like in the village over the hill.' The happy traveller headed off to the next village.

An hour later another traveller walked past. 'Good day sir,' he said, 'I am travelling to the village over the hill. Can you tell me what the people are like there?' 'Well,' said the uncle, 'you've just been to the village on this side of the hill, how did you find the people there?' 'Oh, they weren't friendly at all,' said the traveller. 'Very unwelcoming. I didn't like the village at all.'

'Well, I am sorry to tell you this,' said the uncle, 'but that's how you will find the people in the next village.' The unhappy traveller headed off to the next village.

'Uncle,' said the little boy a little while later, 'to whom did you tell the truth?'

'I told the truth to both of them,' he said. 'The point is, in human relationships, behaviour breeds behaviour.'

Lesson: Show respect for people and you are far more likely to get that same respect back. In human relationships you reap what you sow.

Multiple and emotional intelligences

It is a traditional view that intelligence comes in the obvious forms – knowledge of facts, high IQ, etc. – an expression of the things we have been taught at school. It was believed that we started at some sort of base level and we were vessels into which hard knowledge could be poured. In the early 1980s psychologist Howard Gardner researched what he saw as multiple intelligences. That is to say he believed that intelligence – and therefore 'capabilities' – manifested themselves in many ways. He argued, as have many since, that our education system is designed to fill positions in an educational hierarchy but not for the multifaceted world we now have where a rich variety of knowledge, skills and capabilities are at a premium.

> a rich variety of knowledge, skills and capabilities are at a premium

So, what has this got to do with you and your team colleagues? The answer comes in seeing the value in team colleagues who may be very different from you but who have complementary talents. The team would cease to function very quickly if everyone in the team was cast in your image. The kind of work your team does may be very varied and this means you are going to need a wide variety of 'intelligences' within the team to get your work done. While Howard Gardner initially focused on seven intelligences he acknowledged that there may be hundreds. And they may all have a part to play in the broad spectrum of what we call 'work'.

brilliant example

Here is an example of the way in which a particular kind of 'intelligence' – visual awareness – has become a key workplace skill. Given that we live in a world increasingly given over to visual media – television, the internet, games, sport even – it could be argued that a premium in society and at work should be placed on 'visual awareness'. But at the moment such an intelligence would not be seen as being of prime value in our organisations.

Why should this be so? Possibly because we still value the two traditional intelligences – language and mathematical reasoning – above anything else. These will be important to any team, but in many, visual awareness should be just as highly valued. The method we use to communicate our organisation's messages through inter- and intranets, attract attention to our service and product offerings through different visual media and increasingly use virtual worlds to interact (secondlife.com, for example) means that visual awareness is critical in the modern workplace and in your team.

So this is a very specific example. But think about the multiple 'intelligences' required in a successful sales team or a car manufacturing plant. Or indeed in your own team.

Emotional intelligence

One of the core intelligences required at work – perhaps *the* core desirable 'intelligence' – is what has become known as emotional intelligence (EI). Since the writings of Aristotle it has been recognised that the reading of both your and other's emotions were critical factors in successful human interaction. Daniel Goleman, the man who in recent years has done more to popularise the phrase than anyone else, suggests that there are two key pillars to EI:

1 Personal competence – how we both understand and manage ourselves.

2 Social competence – how we manage relationships with colleagues. (In the case of this book, how we manage relationships within the team.)

In developing relationships, the second of these – social competence – is crucial and a key focus in this chapter. However, to understand the worlds of others in the team it is important to understand and manage your own internal world – the core skill in 'personal competence'.

Personal competence

How self-aware are you? And how accurate and honest is that self-assessment? What are your strengths and vulnerabilities? These are questions that the emotionally intelligent person can answer with reasonable accuracy.

brilliant tip

A crude but fun way to make an assessment of yourself is to imagine that you are selling yourself on eBay. On eBay honesty is essential (to avoid poor feedback which makes it difficult to sell anything on the site in future), so you can put down all the best bits about yourself but you also have to put down all your weaknesses and vulnerabilities. Imagine you are selling your genetic blueprint for future scientific use. What might you say about yourself?

Being self-aware and therefore aware of strengths and vulnerabilities is helpful. But, now being self-aware, should you be looking to 'change' your personality? The answer is no. Your personality gives you a series of character traits. These traits, if you are aware of them, can be adjusted if they damage relationships. It is really about exercising self-control. You can adjust your behaviour. You don't need to change your personality – even if you could.

> self-awareness is really about exercising self-control

The simplest question to ask is: What behaviour will get the most productive outcome in my relations with others in the team? Remembering that you are likely to be working with the team for a substantial period of time; the one-off aggressive outburst might get the result the first time but will damage relationships for a long time after.

Managing yourself

Being self-aware allows you then to manage yourself better. For example, if you find yourself inclined to reject feedback from a team member (perhaps because you are sensitive to criticism) and have acknowledged this to yourself, the next step is to do something about it if you feel you should. But clearly that 'acknowledgement' of the vulnerability comes first.

To take another example, you may find yourself inclined to overreact when team mates make comments that you fundamentally disagree with in meetings. Most of us learn over time that reacting solely with our heart may not be the best way to raise objections. 'Our head' tells us that it might be a more productive approach to let the other person finish, asking questions to check understanding of what has been said and to clarify key points. Only then are you in a position to respond. Self-awareness tells us when our emotions are in danger of hijacking reason and we adjust our behaviour accordingly.

Of course, the less self-aware never learn this – with often damaging consequences.

Social competence

Social competence has two pillars to it, covering your ability to *empathise* with team colleagues – to 'climb' into their world – and your level of *social skills*.

Empathy

Empathy is about how aware we are of the internal minds of others. It is about climbing into individual team colleagues' worlds and knowing how they feel and what they need. When we know this we can adapt our behaviour so it relates to them and the way they see their world. There are two core skills involved and a subset of five additional 'rapport-building' skills. The two underpinning skills are listening and questioning.

Underpinning skill 1 – Listening

The overall mindset

Listening in the context of improving relationships means listening creatively rather than critically. What this means is that you listen with the desire to dig and find out more rather than with the desire to provide an instant critique of what the other person has just said. In previous books, I have called this 'int-erior curiosity' – being curious about what the other person really thinks. It is about wanting to understand rather than immediately respond.

The silent signals: People tell you more if they think you are listening. You send out many 'silent signals' that indicate the degree to which you are listening that the other person, or indeed the team as a whole, will interpret as signs of whether you are listening or not. These include eye contact and open body language.

Asking questions: This is explored in the next section.

Whose world? The art of listening means avoiding relating everything the other person says to your own world – as tempting as that can be. Developing relationships in the team means accommodating the opinions and 'world-view' of team mates, and to do this you need to climb into their world – not superimpose your world on theirs.

Underpinning skill 2 – Questioning

Use the following four-step approach to understand people better and what they are thinking:

1   *The WHs*: The 'who, what, why, where, when, how' questions are the best questions for getting people to open up.

2   *Probing*: These dig a bit deeper once initial information has been established. 'I was particularly interested…', 'I wanted to ask you about that' and 'You mentioned… is that something that is particularly important to you… why do you say that?' are all good probing style questions.

3   *Clarifying*: This is a more closed style of question geared to getting a specific response. 'I want to be sure I have understood you…' and 'Are you saying…' are examples of this style.

4   *Closing*: Questions where we seek a definitive 'yes' or 'no' response. These are best asked towards the end of an interaction. They are not good information gathering questions. 'Are you happy to work with me on the project, in the light of what we have said?' 'Shall we meet at 4pm tomorrow after we've had time to absorb what we've discussed?' These questions get the desired 'yes' or 'no' reply.

'Reading' people

As we seek to get to know people better, team mates or others, and find out what they think and feel, they often leak signals of discomfort or indeed signals that they are comfortable. Not only can you read these discomfort 'leak' signals yourself but you can develop complementary skills that put colleagues at ease in your company.

> develop complementary skills that put colleagues at ease

This section suggests some of the 'leak' signals that you can 'read' followed by positive rapport-building approaches you can use.

brilliant tip

People are not as straightforward as they seem. They might be saying 'yes' to you but inside they are really thinking 'no'. Use your intuition here. If you feel this might be the case look out for 'leak' signals that demonstrate that the mouth is saying one thing while the mind is thinking another. We actually aren't that good at hiding what we think but it needs an effort to read the signs.

Here are some factors to consider.

Body language

- *Discomfort* – Repetitive actions such as leg crossing. Touching parts of the face regularly. Clenching fists. Discomfort/unease often reveals itself in body language clusters – a series of revealing actions and gestures.

- *Rapport building* – Open posture, palms open. No pointing or gesticulating. Avoid regular body posture changes because this signals your own unease. Face the other person but just slightly to the side.

Voice

- *Discomfort* – Passive, timid voice or aggressive and loud voice. Truncated speech. Loss of conversational fluency.

- *Rapport building* – Clear, concise. Use pauses to allow others to speak and to allow them time to absorb what you have said.

Eyes

- *Discomfort* – Moving the eyes away indicates discomfort or unease (e.g. looking away to a point at or near to the ground). Closing the eyes – even momentarily – indicates that you have hit a very raw nerve.

- *Rapport building* – Make regular eye contact 60–70 per cent of the time but not continuously. Use a point 1–3 cms above the eyes (i.e. middle of the forehead) or the bridge of the nose the rest of the time so that the other person does not feel they are in a stare-out.

Physiognomy

- *Discomfort* – The face 'leaks' many signs of comfort or discomfort. Red face, sweating, biting lip, raised veins on temples, a tightening of facial muscles all indicate unease or worse.

- *Rapport building* – A tough one. If you can control your 'leak' signals then you may have spent time as a Buddhist monk or similar!

Others

- *Discomfort* – A series of gestures may indicate tension. Tie straightening in men, continuous grooming, tapping the floor with the shoe or being distracted by physical objects are all signs of tension.

- *Rapport building* – Keep still. Let colleagues know that your attention is focused on them and only them.

brilliant tip

When people feel discomfort they may hide their feelings or they may react in ways that are not normal for them. Because these reactions are likely to be emotional it can be easy to think that this person is 'emotional/unprofessional' but they may well be emotional because they care more than you.

Knowing your team mates better

You get to know people better if you work on the assumption that there are 7 billion worlds out there. Formulating 'first impressions' can blind you from seeing that there may be more to a team mate than you first saw. Here are some of the dangers of instant categorisation followed by productive actions.

> formulating 'first impressions' can blind you

1 Shall we dance?

If someone believes that you or others perceive them in a certain way they may well try to live up to the image. They will often stereotype themselves – performing the role or category they think they are expected to perform. Here are a few examples:

- '*She's a bit mad*' – So I try to do wacky things because that is what the team expects of me.

- '*You're great in a crisis*' – So I am compelled to clear up the mess every time there's a big problem.

- '*He doesn't have a lot of ideas*' – So I keep quiet in meetings for fear that I would be ignored if I said something anyway.

2 The 'hardening of the categories'

Educationist and creativity writer Mark Brown (whose work is referred to regularly in this book) came up with the memorable phrase 'hardening of the categories' to illustrate the way in which we can easily stereotype people as we develop relationships with them – particularly in the early stages of team development. We take a mental photo early on based on one or two assumptions (maybe someone told us something about them) or because we saw them do something that confirmed the category or stereotype we had attached to them initially. Once the category has been implanted in the mind we then look out for the behaviour that reinforces the category and ignore all the pointers that suggest the person is not the person you initially assumed them to be. Hence the 'hardening of the categories'.

3 Mini-me

Falling into the trap of only valuing those with whom you agree is common: what has been called the 'mini-me' syndrome. Many people have just a select few categories into which they place people. The first category (1) contains those people with whom you find yourself in regular agreement – and they tend to be 'like me'. There are then three or four other categories into which we dump everyone else. And of course because they are 'less like me' we tend not to take category 2 to 5 people as seriously.

brilliant dos and don'ts

Do

✔ See first impressions as no more than initial, vague ideas about people because that, in reality, is all they are.

✔ Seek contrary evidence that may challenge that initial first impression. People are far more complex than any first impression can convey.

✔ Explore the uniqueness of team mates rather than assuming that they fit neatly into one of a few limiting categories. They will value the fact that you see them as a unique individual.

Don't

✗ Be a slave to a personality profile. Any 'personality profiling' done around the team should be taken as no more than an interesting diversion. People are far deeper, more complex and interesting than any 'profile' might suggest.

Social skills

The second pillar to 'social competence' are your social skills or what Daniel Goleman refers to in this context as 'your adeptness at introducing desirable responses in others'. There is considerable overlap with 'empathy' here in that a number of the attributes required to be empathic are also invaluable inthis second pillar – particularly the universal skills of listening and questioning.

These social skills are essential to the team because they elicit positive responses to everyday team challenges. They include the following.

Managing conflict

This is your ability to ease disagreement and discord when it threatens both team harmony and the work of the team. It needs to be emphasised that a degree of conflict can be good for a team as it can be a useful instrument in change and innovation.

Assertiveness, persuasion and influencing

This is where you seek agreed, mutually productive outcomes in interactions with other team members. Empathy is essential in helping you do this. Failure to reach out and understand the viewpoints of others turns these three 'win-win' based approaches into success through bullying and force. They may work once or twice for you but over time they damage relationships within the team.

Collaboration

The more emotionally intelligent team members will recognise that, although it is unreasonable for all team members to be number one on each other's Christmas card lists, there is no reason why they should not be able to unite in pursuing the shared goals of the team. Take an example like The Beatles back in the 1960s. Rampant egos and regular disagreements, particularly in their 'middle years', created a frisson in the band and yet they were still able to generate their best music because they stayed focused on producing great music together. The break-up happened

> unite in pursuing the shared goals of the team

when three of them wanted to pursue their own agendas by becoming overly competitive, which made it impossible to operate as a group any more.

Confidence building

Your range of social skills will include helping team members to maximise their capabilities. This is not just a team leadership role – it should be part of the culture of the team. Think of the way that sports teams constantly gee each other up, patting themselves on the back, congratulating themselves on success, praising good performance, offering a shoulder when things don't go as planned. They do it because it works.

Situational sensing

Your skills in managing conflict, showing empathy and engendering collaboration will come from what is known by practitioners in emotional and social intelligence as 'situational sensing'. Here you are able to sense what is happening around you from both an individual and a group perspective, and adapt your behaviour so that outcomes are productive. Of course, these skills cannot suddenly appear in you overnight. Some people seem to have them naturally, others have to work very hard at them. What is important is that anyone who has a desire to sense situations better has already started to do so because their antennae have woken up and tuned into what is going on around them. The desire to change the way you see the world – and, closer to home, the way you see your team mates – is a vital first step.

brilliant tip

Say one of your team is struggling with a particular task that you are able to perform. Jumping in and performing a perfect demonstration may make the situation worse as you remind that person of their perceived (but misplaced) inadequacy. You can begin by showing a bit of empathy instead: 'It was a bit like that for me too the first few times I tried it. Don't worry, we all struggled a bit at first. What I found was that if I did xxx then things got a bit easier.'

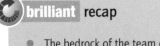 **recap**

- The bedrock of the team comprises the ground *rules*, the acknowledgement of individual *rights* and the *respect* that team members show for each other.
- Self-knowledge and an awareness of the feelings, needs and concerns of team colleagues provide a firm basis for strong team relationships.
- Explore the uniqueness of each person in the team.
- Listening and questioning are the essential underpinning skills in relationship building.
- Avoid categorisation of team mates. Try to understand the unique world in which your team mate lives.
- Work out approaches that will give the best chance of mutually productive outcomes.

The team that learns together

Experience comes from bad judgement. Good judgement comes from experience.

Your team's knowledge has to grow in order for it to deal with current problems in new ways and to increase its capacity to deal with the future (what is known in some circles as 'capacity building'), otherwise it runs the risk of failure. The primary concern in this section on team learning is to look at what the team can do now to deal with current challenges – the here and now. Your team needs to learn in this instance to:

- provide solutions to existing problems;
- learn from past experience;
- avoid the repetition of mistakes; and
- plan for the future.

So far this chapter on relationships has presented many of the skills needed in creating a dynamic team that learns together – listening, questioning, an empathic mindset, an awareness of your own strengths and vulnerabilities. However, before your team develops a learning culture it does need to develop some rules around which the team will learn.

brilliant dos and don'ts

Learning as a team requires you personally, and the team as a whole, to commit to the following:

Do

✔ Acknowledge that the solutions to current problems and the strategies to deal with them will often come from the team itself. Your team, however, is wise enough to bring in outside advice if it needs to.

✔ Make sure that the team focuses on team performance and team issues as a whole. However, in an environment where relationships are strong in the team, team members, including you, should be welcoming feedback and critique on their own performance.

✔ Have open discussion about the challenges your team faces as a unit. Part of the process of learning means that team members will need to be honest about problems and challenges they may be having.

✔ Remember that what gets said in the team stays in the team. The whole world can know and benefit from what your team has learned but the team keeps to itself the personal issues involved (such as team conflicts and disagreements) on the journey there.

Don't

✘ Draw attention to what you feel are others' personality failings. Statements such as 'You're just not tough enough John' destroy personal confidence and team relationships.

✘ Ignore opportunities for the team to review progress and learn from what has been done.

You, your learning and your team – some different approaches

There are three approaches to team learning explored in this section:

1 A form of 'action learning' where you and the team deal with a particular, current problem.

2 Where the team uses the GROW model collectively to improve.

3 Where you ask the team for feedback on your performance.

Action learning

One of the great heroes of learning in organisations is the late Reg Revans. A visionary before his time he saw the value of what he called 'action learning' and espoused it in a number of books and articles. His thoughts on how we learn at work are now being embraced around the world, particularly where teams have a greater degree of autonomy. It is a great tool for problem solving where the answers are not apparent.

> action learning is a great tool for problem solving

Revans argues that action learning is a combination of two forces:

1 *Programmed (Knowledge)*. This comprises the knowledge you have internalised that will help you operate in situations where there is a single answer – and you know what that answer is. The word 'programmed' – although somewhat clinical – acknowledges that you are already 'wired' with the required knowledge.

2 *(Insightful) Questioning*. As many have said, learning is not just a matter of sitting back and absorbing information. It is much more an active process and it begins with asking the right kind of questions or what Revans refers to as 'insightful questions'. It's a bit like the best doctors who don't take symptoms at face

value but instead ask deeper, investigative questions that get to the root cause of an illness. A better diagnosis and cure are therefore found. Indeed the problem may be very different from the one initially envisaged.

brilliant definition

Action learning

The basis of action learning is represented by the formula $L = P + Q$ or:

(Action) Learning = Programmed (Knowledge) + (Insightful) Questioning

Action learning is a non-specific activity – Reg Revans argues that if you could articulate it clearly then it would cease to be 'action learning' in that all situations are different and the lines of insightful questioning are dependent on the nature of the problem. There is, however, a six-step process that can be followed.

Step 1: The problem
The problem is presented by the relevant person (and it could be you) to the team. The problem owner needs to remain accessible to the team but can decide not to be a part of the discussion. If this is you, ask the team for an opinion. It is essential that the problem is a very real one. Action learning is about immediate action once an answer has been identified.

Step 2: What is the problem?
This is the stage where insightful questioning is crucial. The problem may well be different from that which is presented by the problem owner but only deep insightful questioning will reveal this. The problem may be symptomatic of something bigger, which should now become the priority problem. The problem may need to be reframed in order that appropriate answers are generated. Here is a classic and much-quoted example of re-framing.

A team of architects were trying to work out where to put the footpaths surrounding an office block and were struggling to come up with answers. Instead they re-framed the problem and asked: 'Where do the office workers want to walk?' After asking that question they decided to wait six months to see where the office workers actually did walk and then laid tarmac where the grass was most heavily trodden.

What was great about this problem was that they didn't even need to answer their own insightful question.

Step 3: Defining the problem goal

Once insightful questioning has revealed the true nature of the problem, the problem goal (for which solutions are needed) can then be clearly defined.

Step 4: Identifying actions

Again, insightful questioning and inquiry are needed to create a range of possible solutions to deal with the problem goal. This is a bit like the classic tool of finding 100 right answers rather than just 1.

Step 5: Decision and action

Once a range of possible actions have been identified the team can then start to reach some decisions. It may be that with some of the identified actions the team as a whole, or a team member, can try to implement them to see how they work (the less risky). Success or failure will create a learning experience for the team.

Ultimately, the team will identify a way forward. It may be, however, that the way forward does not work as envisaged, in which case a return to step 2 will be required.

Step 6: What have we learned?

This step is crucial but often missed by teams. If the team has helped the individual or the team itself solve the problem it is crucial that the team identifies what it has learned from the whole process. Ask questions such as: 'What have we learned that will help us improve as a team and individuals?', 'What have we learned that can be shared with other teams and departments?' and 'What would we do differently next time?'

You will find the chapter on creative problem-solving teams (Chapter 10) particularly useful in your exploration of action learning and how to apply it. Look out for the approaches to team ideas generation.

Team 'GROW'th – building capability

John Whitmore, coaching expert, devised a very simple acronym for both individual and team development known as the 'GROW' model – Goals, Reality, Options, Will. It is an acronym used for coaching, mostly as a means of motivating individuals to learn when being 'coached'. In our context it is used for building the knowledge capacity and capability of the team.

GROW – Goals, Reality, Options, Will

In the modern organisation, teams are usually assembled on the basis that each person brings complementary knowledge and skills to the team that are identified as essential in the team's work both now and in the near future. However, knowledge that is kept in the hands of a small number of people – or maybe even one person – is dangerous for the team and also frustrating for individual team members who see little potential for personal growth. Think how you feel, for example, when you have little idea what is going on when others clearly do.

In the modern team there is little scope for protectionism around your own area of work. You need to be alive to the fact that you should be sharing with team members your approaches to your work and also be open enough to appreciate that there may be other ways of doing it. The GROW approach is very useful in coaching team members to achieve team goals, but the model acknowledges that the methods identified for reaching personal and team goals are in the hands of the learner.

Where do we want to get to? (the goal)

If the team is clear on where it is trying to get to (where the goal is an imperative) then this merely needs to be a restatement of the objective: 'We need to do x to get here and we need to get here because...' In other instances, the learner will have a greater degree of motivation to learn if they can devise their learning goals with you.

Where are we now? (the reality)

What is your existing knowledge and skill level (point A), and what is the gap between where we are now and where you need to get to, to achieve the goal (point B)?

What possibilities are open to us? (the options)

It is essential that this is an open dialogue between you and the person who is learning (and you should be learning all the time too!). In other words, a variety of options should be discussed – and in the best possible world as many of those options as possible should be presented – that will get the person from point A to point B.

Are we committed to the journey to achieve the goal? (the will)
Almost anyone will be more committed to that journey if they have
been part of the process of deciding how the journey will be done.
It may be that the journey needs to be done in a very specific way
with a very specific end goal. That shouldn't matter. The important
point is that when you share knowledge with your team colleagues
so that they can improve, this should be done as a two-way process.
It is not just about you telling them what to do. It is about both
parties: asking questions; exploring possibilities; being open to
other approaches ('How might you go about it?'); sharing your
experiences ('When I did this it was disastrous because...'); and the
learner seeing a point to the learning.

Feedback

 **example**

James's story

I work in the legal profession and we start with a reasonably high opinion
of ourselves given the rigorous training we go through to get where we are.
I think just to start giving feedback and expect it to be accepted is naive –
particularly in an environment like ours.

Our team approached it in an interesting way. We sat down and discussed
how we might give feedback to each other – peer-to-peer. We agreed a
set of ground rules around which feedback should be given. Just the very
act of agreeing a set of ground rules immediately made us all more open
to the idea that it was an acceptable thing to do. I must emphasise that
there has to be a belief within the team that feedback will enhance team
performance: it will help you get better. If team members don't believe that
then there is little point in going through with it. So perhaps this is the
place where any discussion about feedback begins – will it help the team
improve? And how will it help us improve? Go from there.

As James's story illustrates the best way for your team to embrace feedback is for the team to agree to develop a culture of giving and receiving feedback between team members: team members need to see the value to them personally and then to the team. Some are more receptive to feedback than others. When developing a culture of feedback in the team understand that the process may be 'two steps forward, one step back' because feedback can touch sensitivities.

feedback can touch sensitivities

That said, it is a crucial tool in team learning. The team that does not embrace it does not move forward.

brilliant tip

Be aware of how team members might respond to feedback, even if the team has agreed to a feedback culture within it – emotions are involved here. The feedback might cover something that the individual was aware of but didn't think anyone else was. Or it might be a bolt from the blue to them.

So who do you learn from at work?

- Anyone who you have respect for who is more senior than you (but definitely not those you have no or little respect for). That might be the team leader, a manager or other people outside your direct circle.

- Your peers (and in the context of this chapter this is the most important group). It is why strong relationships between you and your peers are not just important in great team working but also in great team learning.

Where you have respect for your peers in the team you should welcome the opportunity to ask them for feedback on your performance. There is one initial caveat here:

Feedback should be sought for the most genuine of reasons. Not because you want compliments or you want to use the feedback as a convenient way of highlighting others' – as you see it – inadequacy. You seek because you want to learn.

brilliant dos and don'ts

When asking for feedback from the team the following is useful advice:

Do

✔ Thank the giver.

✔ Listen and try to understand what others are saying. Do this by:

- Seeking specific information. Feedback is often given vaguely. Seek specific examples – but do not do this in a *prove it to me* way.

- Continually searching for clarity.

- Not offering opinions on what is being said – agreement or disagreement. You are seeking information.

✔ Thank the giver or givers of the feedback and then ask:

- Have others said similar things to you? Are there patterns to the feedback you have been getting?

- How the feedback is useful to you and how you can use it if it is.

Don't

✘ Be defensive by arguing or continually justifying yourself.

✘ Ignore feedback – use it.

When a team member asks for feedback

If your team has a culture in place where feedback is an accepted tool for individuals to learn from the team, the job of giving feedback will be easier. Nonetheless feedback isn't about telling people what you think of them and what they did. There are sensitivities involved – and some rules to follow.

Perhaps the best initial approach when asked for feedback is to reflect the question back first. If there is criticism to be done it is much the best approach to invite self-critique first. Why?

- We act best on what we realise for ourselves rather than what we are just 'told'.
- The person is often overly self-critical and may well be surprised when the team expresses surprise itself that an individual has raised a particular issue. This gives an opportunity for praise for the things that were well done and makes the person much more alive when the conversation turns to areas for improvement. Praise and room for improvement should go together in a feedback conversation.

Then:

- Concentrate on those things you know to be true, i.e. not heresay or half-baked notions.
- Give specific examples where necessary to back this up.
- Always encourage a conversation rather than reading off a checklist of stuff done badly.
- Always gear the conversation to the individual trying to work out the answers for themselves.

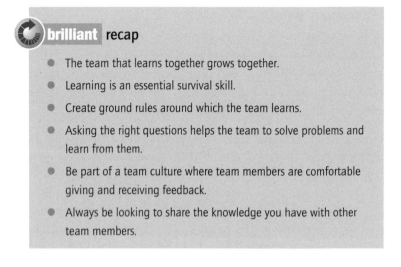

brilliant recap

- The team that learns together grows together.

- Learning is an essential survival skill.

- Create ground rules around which the team learns.

- Asking the right questions helps the team to solve problems and learn from them.

- Be part of a team culture where team members are comfortable giving and receiving feedback.

- Always be looking to share the knowledge you have with other team members.

In the early part of this chapter an emphasis was placed on self-awareness: understanding your strengths and vulnerabilities, how your emotions work for you, etc. In the next chapter this knowledge will be invaluable as you seek to understand what roles you perform in the team. Not only is self-awareness an internal thing, it is also about how you understand your position in the wider world and, in the case of the next chapter, within your team.

CHAPTER 3

What's in a brilliant team?

A team is a small number of people with complementary skills who are committed to a common purpose, set of performance goals, and approach for which they hold themselves mutually accountable.

Katzenbach and Smith, *The Wisdom of Teams*

If you are to be part of a brilliant team you need to be clear about the role you perform in delivering team goals. You also need to be clear about, and value, the roles that other team members are performing. This chapter is divided into four sections that will help you and your team colleagues do this. These are:

1 The core roles that need to be performed in any successful team – *Team roles.*

2 How you can perform your 'role' better – *You and your team role.*

3 How you can work better with team members who are performing particular roles – *Working with other 'roles'.*

4 A short case study that illustrates how clearly defined roles can deliver a brilliant team performance – *Team roles and brilliant performance.*

Team roles

Brilliant teams are not created in laboratories and just occasionally they come together by chance. But putting some thought into what roles the team needs to perform makes 'chance' redundant. Lots of research has been put into what it takes to build a brilliant team. Perhaps one of the best attempts to assess team roles was by business thinker and writer Peter Honey. He came up with four universal roles that he felt needed to be performed in a successful team. The four are:

---

brilliant teams are not created in laboratories

---

1   Leaders.

2   Doers.

3   Thinkers.

4   Carers.

You may want to add to this list by thinking of roles that relate to the individual circumstances of your own team. You could also add a fifth role – 'achievers' – because none of the roles above, in themselves, guarantees achievement. However, I feel that all four of these roles have achievement written into their DNA if the roles are performed well, in that a high-performing team needs all of the roles to be performed to succeed. The doers may be the obvious achievers but there is no guarantee that they 'do' the right thing.

Although Peter Honey has expanded and amended his initial four roles, and other thinkers such as Meredith Belbin have developed their own, these four are a very sensible base point from which to start.

brilliant definitions

Here are the definitions of these four critical roles.

Leader

Leaders create vision, direction and purpose and are decisive when they need to be. The leader or leaders in the team may well not just be the designated leader (the manager of the group) – others may perform leadership roles. Team leadership is covered in the next chapter of this book.

Doer

The doers are committed to action. They see the ways to do things first before considering the pitfalls (if they consider the pitfalls at all). This positive spirit can be infectious. When the team sees someone in the team getting things done, team members get inspired to follow, although for others it has the opposite effect (reminding them, so they erroneously believe, of their own inadequacies).

The 'can do, will do' people are essential if the team is going to achieve anything. The team relies on them to run with the team's ideas. So doers get stuff done. However, I believe there is a subcategory of 'doer' – achiever. Doers get stuff done but achievers get the right stuff done.

Thinker

The thinkers are the idea generators and the potential problem solvers in the team. They may be voluble but it is more likely that they are quiet and contemplative. The thinkers can act like a 'team helicopter', hovering above a situation, making an assessment of that situation and considering a range of possible alternatives to deal with it. They often also act as a valuable counterweight to the energetic doers.

Carer

The carers generate team cohesion through growing strong relationships within the team. The carer's role is often a subtle, less obvious one. But it is a critical one. Teams need emotional glue – a bind that keeps them together through the challenges, the conflicts, the disagreements and the stresses of day-to-day working.

Because the carers are concerned with relationships they are also essential in building the bonds that must exist between the team and those that the team serves. This role is so important because all teams have a purpose that transcends an internal function.

Human beings are complex. Teams rightly identify the need to have ideas and put those ideas into action. But when human beings are involved things are not as straightforward as this. The 'carers' are able to understand the complexity of interpersonal relationships and get to the core of what makes a harmonious working environment.

You, the team and team roles

This section looks first at you and the role or roles you perform ('What am I?') and then at team roles from the perspective of the team as a whole ('What's in a team?').

What am I?

It is likely that you are already thinking about the role you perform in your team. Leader, doer, thinker or carer? Perhaps you are saying to yourself that you perform more than one of those roles regularly? Or the role you perform depends on the nature of the work being done. As you consider these roles in your own work you may find the following points useful.

More than one role?

You are unlikely to perform one of these roles to the exclusion of the others. If you were to allocate 100 points across the four roles, as you assess your work in the team in its totality, how many would you allocate to each of them?

Can I offer more?

Widen the range of what you can offer to the team. You probably have a disposition to perform a particular role but in certain situations you may well assume other roles too.

What have I done in the past?

Think about teams you have been part of in the past and consider the roles you have performed in those teams. Use the four as a base point but do expand on them for your own purposes. Getting an idea about how you respond in different circumstances can be useful in helping you to understand what performance roles you might take on as the team undertakes its work.

'I am as I am'

You may be performing a particular role because you or others have assumed that you have a particular character trait. For example, you may be a quieter, more reflective type and therefore behave according to that self-perception in a team environment. But there are plenty of 'quiet achievers' around –

> there are plenty of 'quiet achievers' around

people who go about the team's business with the minimum of fuss and get the job done. Challenge the assumptions that you and others may be making about yourself.

Room for growth

The roles of the team should be based on the skills and capabilities of team members. But capabilities in this case can also refer to 'capabilities yet to be developed'. You can learn to think better just as you can learn to lead and learn to develop stronger relationships. So even though the history lesson says you tend to perform a particular role within a team, do not limit yourself for ever to that role.

What's in a team?

This section looks at roles in the team as a whole rather than your own individual roles.

brilliant tip

To help you think about how these roles apply, take a team with which you are familiar but not a part of – a sports team you support, a society perhaps or a team at work in another section or department. Who performs the four key roles in those teams? (Note: don't make the assumption that the team manager/ co-ordinator performs the leadership role all of the time – see the next chapter.) Does the team perform well? If it doesn't is it because one of the four key roles isn't being performed well? If the team is a good one what can you learn from the way they work?

Assumption challenging

You cannot always make assumptions that certain people will take up certain roles because they normally do. For example, there are plenty of doers who get on with the job but who seem to become paralysed when a high-pressure or crisis situation develops. It may well be that in a crisis other members of the team emerge who seem able to get stuff done when the crisis situation demands it. Don't therefore underestimate the capacity of others in the team to perform in ways that pleasantly surprise you.

'Role dumping'

Saying 'Ed is always great in a crisis' is not particularly fair on the 'doer' Ed if all Ed gets to deal with are serious problems. Ed may quite like this flattery for a while but may begin to wonder why he is seen only as a crisis problem solver. Just as Ed needs to grow into other areas of the team's work, other people in the team need to be able to operate in Ed's traditional territory too. Remember the gruesome 'London Bus' scenario: 'What would we do if Ed fell under a London bus tomorrow?'

Team balance

If your team isn't working as it should be, the reasons may be complex – Chapter 9 refers to a number of key reasons why teams can fail. However, it may just be because the functions associated with these four core roles are not being performed. Perhaps team harmony is not as it should be because there is no one assuming that caring role. Maybe the team is stagnating because not enough new ideas are coming out. Maybe your meetings are great talking shops but no one really does anything afterwards (very common). With those common problems comes a solution – serious consideration of the 'balance' of the team and the roles that need to be performed to create that balance. Do not underestimate them.

You and your team role

This section covers three of the four roles (doer, thinker and carer) and is devised to help you perform each of these roles better. The fourth role, leader, is covered in Chapter 4.

When you are a 'doer'

Does it deliver the team goal?

Make the connection between what you are doing and what the team is trying to do. Random actions can be damaging. Action that directly connects to the goals of the team gets the results the team desires. Getting stuff done is not the same as getting the right stuff done.

> random actions can be damaging

Learning to pace yourself

It can be frustrating when others do not operate at the same speed as you. Sometimes that frustration may be justified, but do ask if they are offering an invaluable counterweight to your own ill-considered haste.

brilliant tip

Festina lente or 'make haste slowly' was the old mantra of the Fabian Society in the nineteenth century. Sometimes we need to slow down to let people or events catch up with us.

Sharing the credit

Doers are the people who may get more credit than the rest of the team because they are the obvious achievers in the eyes of others. Those reading this who have the doer's disposition must be prepared to share the credit – even if you are in the limelight. Both the team members and the team's leader should value the contribution of all team members. The doers didn't do it all by themselves.

Ask for help

Because 'doers' are associated with action and activity they may not admit they are struggling. There is no prize for heroic failure when the help others could have given was not asked for or utilised. Sometimes doers need to suppress ego if it means that the job is going to get done.

When you are a 'thinker'

Make a contribution

Potential contributions to team discussions that remain in your head are pointless. Be prepared to make a contribution. If you don't value your thoughts and ideas it is not reasonable to expect others to do so.

Be positive in your contribution

Thinkers are also good problem forecasters and this can be a valuable defence mechanism against ill thought out action (often initiated by the doers). But you do need to strike a balance between sounding out warnings and killing off the energy and vitality in the team. Saying 'we can't do this because' all the time sucks the life out of the team. While there are bad ideas and actions that should be avoided you may often find that, on closer inspection, it is only 20 per cent of an idea that needs to be tweaked to make it workable rather than just confining an idea or suggestion to the dustbin.

Use your 'thinker' skills to make refinements rather than dustbin confinements.

Welcome the challengers

Don't be put off because others disagree with your thoughts and ideas. Ideas become stronger with rigorous debate.

Learn to collaborate

If you feel that your thoughts and ideas might meet resistance seek out possible allies first. Perhaps get others in the team to introduce your ideas first so that the team sees a wider base of support.

When you are a 'carer'

You are the 'glue'

You provide the emotional glue of the team – recognising the value of strong relationships within the team and cementing them. You repair relationships and bonds. You recognise that a harmonious team is a healthy team.

Conflict can be good

As a 'carer' you will have a disposition to ease conflict. However, recognise too that managed conflict and disagreement is a necessary instrument of deeper insight and ultimately change. The key here is to be happy with disagreement but not with a disagreeable approach that others may use when they disagree.

Use your 'emotional intelligence'

Use the skills that come naturally to you – mediation, empathy, listening and questioning, for example

_____
use the skills that come naturally to you
_____

– to ease personality clashes, to listen to team members with problems and to repair long-standing wounds in the team. These skills come under the umbrella of what we call 'emotional intelligence' – see Chapter 2.

Working with other 'roles'

Working with 'doers'

These are some of the challenges that doers in the team *may* present to the rest of the team. Do not assume this about doers *per se*. Plenty of doers focus and channel their actions clearly and directly. These are some of the things that *some* doers can be inclined to do *some* of the time. Certainly not all doers – and certainly not all of the time either.

Keep the doers focused

- *The challenge*: While the doers get things done, do they get the right things done? Are they like the pumped up balloon which, when its gas gets released, fires randomly around the room and then expires on the floor? Or, the driver of the car who keeps driving even when they don't know where they are heading and haven't got a map?

- *A solution*: Make sure the team has clear goals and objectives that doers understand, agree with and can act on. This is not just the role of the designated team leader. We all have a responsibility to keep the 'rightness' of our direction.

The boring stuff needs to be done too!

- *The challenge*: Doers don't necessarily like bureaucracy. This can be good because they have a mindset that seeks to look at breaking bureaucratic systems. But it can be counter-productive if critical 'process-based' work is being missed. Safety and legality are two such examples.

- *A solution*: There are, of course, plenty of action people who recognise the need for systems and procedures. But there are plenty who aren't the best at the administrative side of things. In this situation the team needs to take an important call. Will it stunt the energy of the doers to push them into a more procedural direction? Do we have people in the team who can and are willing to pick up the administrative shortfall?

  Everyone in the team needs to understand where the administrative/procedural rules can be stretched a little and where the rules must be followed to the letter. As mentioned earlier, safety and legality cannot be violated and neither can business ethics and morality.

Keep the doers flexible

- *The challenge*: The doers can be inflexible and see their way as the only way. They go ahead and do it anyway without considering the possibility that there are alternatives or that sometimes to 'make haste slowly' is best.

- *A solution*: Team meetings should contain rigorous debate and a clear think through of the key issues before actions are *agreed*. If you feel that the team is not discussing the issues properly you can take on the role of challenger – though this must be done non-confrontationally.

Keep the doers active

- *The challenge*: Doers are active people and may create activity where none exists. This includes starting fires so that they can get busy putting them out.

- *Some solutions*: Doers need action to keep them interested. Keep the doers active, keep their horizons broad, keep their goals challenging. Doers like to be stretched. But be sure that the actions of the doers are in line with the goals of the team. Are the doers clear about where they have freedom to act and where they need to act in a more controlled manner?

Doers often do stuff even if nobody is watching anyway. This is great (as long as the actions are not destructive) – it creates a sense of energy and vitality round the team.

Doers can be terrific team ambassadors because they are high profile – they are your tendrils out into the world beyond the team. But be sure that what the doers are saying and doing are the things that the team wants the doers to be saying and doing.

Working with 'thinkers'

Opening up the thinkers

- *The challenge*: Thinkers may 'live in their head' and may therefore not be as forthcoming with their views as others in the team. Sometimes quieter team members do not get heard. Their quietness is assumed to mean they have nothing to offer. You need to open up the thinkers.

- *A solution*: Encourage the quiet – they may have insights that others have not considered. It is tempting to say that the thinkers are not being held back in your team, but how do you know?

Rigorous debate

- *The challenge*: Thinkers can however be the opposite – dominating, willing their views on the team, perhaps even taking an aggressive rather than assertive approach when they feel others aren't sharing the same enthusiasm for their thoughts.

- *A solution*: In this situation, counter-argument, rigorous talking through of ideas and getting a variety of perspectives without quelling the energy of the dominating ideas people is key. Above all, those who are providing a counterweight to the dominant thinkers should keep their cool.

Thinking too much

- *The challenge*: Thinkers are often good at seeing 'the bigger picture'. They can take a helicopter view of what is really going on – something they share with good leaders. However, to add a bit of healthy contradiction here, some thinkers can get locked too far into the opposite of this – the minutiae – and as a consequence struggle to break out of a limited perspective.

- *A solution*: Where analysis paralyses team momentum it is incumbent on other team members to emphasise the need for action. At some point, analysis has to stop and action begin. In the final analysis, action of any kind – within reason – will usually be better than team inertia. Analysis can often mean that we talk ourselves out of doing the right thing as well as the wrong thing.

Working with 'carers'

As carers are likely to be the least-valued team members this section emphasises the importance of this role.

Listen to the carers

Because 'carers' are multi-sensory they are a good conduit to the outside world. They can intuit that relations between the team and others (with customers, for example) are not as good as they could be and are able to provide an early-warning system. Are you listening to them?

A life without the carers

If you need convincing about the value of the carers, think about the 'carers' in your team or in teams you have worked in previously. What might the team have looked like if they weren't there? What would relationships have been like? Would it have been as enjoyable? Would team productivity have suffered?

Team well-being

Of all the roles this is the one that is the most underestimated (being seen by some as a bit 'soft and fluffy'). This role has the same value as the others, but it is tempting to say that 'ideas' (thinkers) and 'action' (doers) are more important because they are more tangible. The carer's role is tough to perform but essential to the well-being of the team.

Team roles and brilliant performance

▶ brilliant example

Frankie, George, Christian, Kevin and Peter worked the hardest. Frankie would start the rolling climbs, setting a strong tempo and dropping riders. When Frankie got tired, George would pull and a few more riders would fall by the wayside, unable to keep our pace. Then came Tyler who would pick up the pace, dropping even more of our competitors. Finally, I would be left with Kevin, pulling me through the steeps. In that way we whittled down the field.

Lance Armstrong, *It's Not About the Bike*

This chapter has looked at the four universal team roles. Teams also need a blend of skills based on the more specific capabilities of each team member that allow them to get the work of the team done. In the quote above the great cyclist Lance Armstrong was able to express what it was the team did to help him to the top of the toughest mountains in Le Tour de France and to ultimate victory (this writer reserves judgement on the 'legalities' connected with the performance of some of the team members!). He focused on the efforts of his team mates – 'les domestiques' – and the roles they had to perform to propel him to the top. Their roles were defined by the skills and capabilities that each rider offered to the team.

In team endurance sports it is known that the 'front-runner' – in this case the lead cyclist – has to work harder than the rest to keep the pace up. Frankie Andreu, a sprinter by inclination, was the man whose skills were most suited to making the early surge through, as Armstrong says, setting the 'strong tempo'. The competitor riders least suited to climbing would soon be dropped. When Andreu got tired (and sprinters generally don't have a lot of stamina) George Hincapie would take over. Having not had to lead the team in the early stages he would have a bit in reserve, as would the next rider to take over at the front after Hincapie, Tyler Hamilton. Kevin Livingstone was usually the last rider with Armstrong as he had the best 'engine' for the latter part of the descent when the field was scattered. And then, finally, if everything had gone to plan, as it usually did, Armstrong would be where he wanted to be – at or as near to the front as he needed to be.

What can your team learn from the above example?

- The team was absolutely clear on its goal.
- It decided what roles needed to be performed to help reach its goal.
- It allocated these roles according to the skills and capabilities of team members.
- Team members were absolutely clear on what their role was in delivering a world-class team performance.
- As Armstrong himself makes clear in his book, much of this was done as a collaborative process between team members and with the input of the team's manager (Johan Bruyneel) who was always able to look at the bigger picture – placing what they were doing in the overall context of the race.

In high-performing teams, team members are able to perform a variety of roles. Perhaps the very best teams bring together a group of people who are able to do, think and care about the team and its activities. And, as we will see in the next chapter, high-performing teams need more than one leader. The team captain in Armstrong's team was not actually Armstrong. Neither was it the team's manager. It was the veteran sprinter Frankie Andreu – the man who got them started on the steep ascents where 'Le Tour' is usually won and lost. He set the tempo by which the rest of the team had to follow.

> high-performing teams need more than one leader

Goal scoring

Once a team goal has been decided and agreed, your team needs to consider what skills are needed within the team to help it realise its goals. In the Lance Armstrong example there was the need for sprinters, climbers, front-runners and cyclists who could pedal a relentless hard pace for a period of time (but not the whole race).

Once the required skills have been assessed teams then need to think about where the gaps lie, and if they can they need to fill them: What capabilities do we have and what do we need?

Questions such as these build up into a four-stage questioning process that will help the team get the right balance of skills it needs to reach its goals:

1   What skills do we need to reach the goal?
2   What are the existing skills within the team?
3   Is there a skills gap and if so how can we fill the gap?
4   Do we have 'back-up' in case of absence, illness or below-par performance from a team member?

brilliant tip

Teams are far more fluid in organisations than they were say 20 or 30 years ago. Where your team is working on a specific project, don't be afraid to look beyond the team for certain skills and capabilities if the requisite knowledge and skills are missing in the team.

Teams operate on dangerous ground when they have knowledge and skills in the hands of only one person. Every opportunity should be taken to share knowledge and skills (see Chapter 2).

brilliant recap

Here are five key points that neatly summarise this chapter:

1 Brilliant teams have a combination of core roles performed by the team members – leader, doer (with added 'achiever' thinker, carer.

2 Consider the role or roles that come most naturally to you in your team and ask what the team is looking for from you in that role.

3 Learn to value the roles that others perform and encourage and support them while they do this.

4 Recognise that a number of other roles (beyond the four identified) need to be performed by the team that will be dependent on the nature of the work being done by the team. Be sure what those roles are in your team and who is performing them. These will be based on the skills of each team member.

5 These additional roles should be built around the specific goals that the team has set.

This chapter has looked at three of the four key roles that Peter Honey suggested needed to be filled in a successful team. The fourth role, the leader, will be the subject of the next chapter. The best leaders may have the characteristics of the doer, thinker and carer within them, and where they don't they need to have the ability to recognise the need for those roles to be performed within the team and to champion those who do so. But, of course, it shouldn't just be leaders who do this. As a team member you should recognise the value that everyone who performs a role brings to the team if they perform it well and particularly when they offer something you don't.

CHAPTER 4

Teams and leadership

Everyone has the capacity to be a leader and has the ability to lead, whether or not they are designated formally as a leader.

John Buchanan, Australian cricket coach

Increasingly, as John Buchanan's quote suggests, we all have to lead whether our job title says we are a leader/manager or not. This chapter looks at the reasons why this is the case and how you can go about doing it well in your team. It is a responsibility many of you assume, no matter how short-term your leadership responsibility lasts. All of you will need to lead in the future. The old maxim – 'When it is necessary to lead, then lead. When it is necessary to be led, be led' – has never been truer.

Brilliant teams also need to be led well by the designated leader. It took us a long time to disconnect the image of the successful leader from the image generated by the old military model: highly directive, even coercive; charging out into the fray; continual exhortations to motivate the troops. The modern team leader now has a range of styles available (the above still being part of the repertoire) – the skill being that the leader recognises when to use which style and with whom.

This chapter looks at the following two elements of teams and leadership in detail:

1 Assuming leadership responsibility when you are not the designated team leader.

2 Looking at the leadership styles available to you when you are the designated team leader.

Leading when you are not 'the leader'

'*There were lots of leaders out on the pitch tonight*' is a part of the regular post-match analysis patter in many sports when the studio experts discuss what the magic formula was that made the winning team successful. The same is increasingly true in our work teams. In this section we look at why this is the case and how you as an individual can fulfil your brief to lead when you need to lead.

Teams need leaders. But it may not be the obvious person who leads the team all the time. The leadership role may not be performed by the 'manager' or the person who sits highest in your organisation's hierarchy. The reason for this is that the leadership role can only be conferred by those being led. A manager can manage ultimately through command and control – although in most situations this should be the last resort management style. A leader cannot resort to hierarchy as the means of controlling the team because leaders rely on such things as respect, trust and sometimes a track record of proven success to give them leadership credibility. Sometimes, someone else in the team has to stand up and lead because the team demands it or because it 'feels' the right thing to do.

> the leadership role can only be conferred by those being led

So, you're not the designated leader but you may well be 'leading'. Why? Are there things you can do to help you in this role? The six reasons listed below are followed by tips to increase effectiveness in this leadership role. You may never have considered yourself as a leader of people or, more specifically, that others in the team look to you to lead at certain points during the team's work. But the chances are they do. And if they haven't yet you can be certain that they will do.

Six reasons why you may be leading the team when you are not the 'designated' leader

1 Your specialist knowledge and skills

Ad hoc teams are regularly brought together to work on particular projects, solve specific problems or explore an issue and make recommendations. You may have been asked to join the team because you have specialist knowledge and skills that will be of benefit to the team. Your specialist knowledge and skills will be frequently called on and when they are you may well be the person whom the others are looking to for direction.

When you have expert knowledge, understand that when you share it others may not grasp this knowledge as quickly as you did. Show patience and remember that they will know things you don't know too. People will remember what you don't tell them (when they find out) as much as they remember what you did tell them. Recognise age gaps and the barriers they can represent (older to younger and vice versa). Younger leaders may have to work harder to get credibility with older groups even if they have the requisite knowledge and skills and quickly generate 'followership' among their own age group.

When you have specialist knowledge or key information it is easy to slip into patronising mode or to play a political game within the team. Very, very occasionally there can be value in holding back in the wider organisation ('the political game') but never to team colleagues – share what you know. Trust will be quickly lost if you don't.

2 Your experience

The team may look to you because you have experienced similar situations currently faced by the team before, or you can see the pitfalls in a particular course of action and are providing an early-warning system for the team which makes it sit up and take notice.

Alternatively, perhaps you were part of a very successful team in the past and the team wants some of that success to 'rub off'. You have the 'aura' of past success!

As a generalisation, younger generations – by which we mean the 'Net Gen' (born after 1977) and Generation 'X' (born after 1964) – are known not to revere experience in the way previous generations might have done. That means that those with experience still have to work hard to earn the respect that they may have assumed they had already earned. These groups are likely to think, 'prove it to me personally'. Experience can still count but it doesn't mean everything any more.

People are very good at talking about failure and many meetings, for example, turn into problem-solving exercises. If you have had previous success, share what it was that made you successful. But try not to become the person that always harks back to the past – 'they were great days, things aren't the same any more'. We can learn from history but don't use it as an opportunity for endless anecdotes.

brilliant tip

There is a difference between being the wise old head and the initiative killing dinosaur ('we can't do this because...' or 'we've done this before, failed, and I don't see how you can do any better'). Use your experience as a vehicle for progress rather than as a means of leading the group into inertia.

3 Your ability to empathise

If you are able to draw yourself into other people's worlds – to understand the world from their perspective – people are very quickly drawn to you. This puts you in a powerful position because team members will feel that they can trust you. You have shown that you have an interest in them and their world and they are more likely to take you seriously as a result.

> team members will feel that they can trust you

brilliant tip

Empathy has to be real. Effective questioning and listening are the key skills here, as was seen in Chapter 2, but action will be the determinant in how empathic you have really been.

4 You can see 'the light'

Where teams are confronted with problems, delicate situations or unforeseen challenges, the person who sees a solution, can express it and secure commitment to that solution is likely to assume some sort of leadership position within the team.

Team members value a clear sense of direction in their personal and working lives, which is why they appreciate those who, in team working, seem to know which path to take.

> **brilliant tip**
>
> It is one thing to be able to see the way ahead for the team but another to be blinded by the light. Keep open to different approaches and ideas as progress is made. An open-mindedness to available options and a willingness to listen and debate mean you will be taken seriously. Those who are inflexible may be seen as arrogant. You cannot be right all of the time.

5 Your technological 'savvy'

Team leaders can lose contact quickly if they fail to understand communication methods favoured by younger members of the team (see Chapter 12). Examples include service engineers or sales people who communicate and problem solve at work via web-based social networking sites ('peer-to-peer' rather than subordinate to manager). New sub-teams may quickly form with a new leadership requirement. Purists may say these are undesirable but the fact is they are inevitable. You may be the leader of the sub-team.

> **brilliant tip**
>
> No purpose is served by being a sub-team that loses contact with the main group or with the designated team leader. In this situation your primary role is to bring teams together and share knowledge and information.

6 Your charisma

Perhaps you have a character that compels others to follow you? Charismatic leaders who generate 'followership' are in a very powerful position because they can get people to unleash extraordinary amounts of energy into the task if they believe in you and the direction you want to take.

brilliant tip

There are plenty of people who use charisma in the most unpleasant of ways – even in the world of business, sport and hobby-based clubs. Charisma comes best served with a number of good human qualities – ethics, morality, concern for others and belief in 'good'. We are not in the world of 'charismatic' dictators or gurus here.

brilliant recap

Leadership capacity within the team

- Brilliant teams require leadership throughout the team – people who can step up and take the team forward when required. If the team is a large one this is essential. We can no longer look to the one person who is the designated leader to do this.

- Teams often need to work at speed, responding to internal and external needs faster, and delivering project work in shorter time-scales. Leaders stimulate this responsiveness.

- Recognise what it is that you bring to the team – when your knowledge and skills are needed you have to be ready to lead the team forward.

- Teams need to be thinking about their internal leadership capacity. Your team needs you to be ready to lead.

Leading when you are the designated leader

If you are the designated leader don't fear pockets of leadership excellence within the team: in fact you should welcome it. Leaders cannot hope to do their job properly without this internal leadership capability.

Using leadership styles

For a leader formally in charge of a team your success is likely to be predicated by two factors:

1 The style of leadership you adopt in a particular situation.
2 The style of leadership you use with each individual in the team.

Some of the most interesting work carried out in the area of leadership styles in the past 20 years has been that done by the Hay Group and subsequently with the input of emotional intelligence proponent Daniel Goleman. Hay Group's research with many thousands of leaders in all kinds of roles around the world has created a link between leaders and their awareness of different styles who are 'cute' enough as leaders to know where and when to apply them. This is strongly grounded in Goleman's work on emotional intelligence – described as your ability to pinpoint your emotions and the emotions of those around you.

Through rigorous research around the world Hay has developed six styles which effective leaders have available to them. This is not just about knowledge of those styles *per se* (although this is important) but which style to adopt in a particular situation and which style to adopt with certain individuals. It is no surprise that one of the original papers Hay published to publicise the styles was called 'Leadership That Gets Results' – the appropriate use of styles gets the job done.

> Hay has developed six styles which effective leaders have available to them

These styles have been amended over the past 10 years, but at the time of writing (2011) Hay's latest research suggests the leader's awareness and appropriate use of the following six styles is critical to individual and team performance:

1 Directive.

2 Visionary.

3 Affiliative.

4 Participative.

5 Pacesetting.

6 Coaching.

Choosing leadership styles: key points

Below is a description of each of the six styles together with advice on their application. Before reading through these there are a few dos and don'ts to consider.

brilliant dos and don'ts

Do

✔ Think carefully about how you have 'led' previously. If you've only really had one or two default styles in the past (not uncommon) you may have to start using the wider repertoire by consciously asking, 'Which style do I need to use here?'

✔ Think about the appropriateness of styles for different situations and different people and weave them into your being. With conscious practice they will become second nature.

Don't

✗ Become a slave to a single style to the exclusion of others. Styles often work in conjunction with each other. Think about which styles might combine well when you are in different situations.

✗ Continually resort to the more command-and-tell approach of the 'directive' style because it is easy. In pressure situations always ask if there is a better style to use. Misuse of this style can be very damaging.

Directive style

This is where the team leader has to adopt a 'do this and do it this way' approach to the team's work. It is easy to dismiss this as an old-fashioned, controlling style of leadership best utilised in the military. In fact only recently has the Hay Group changed the name of this style from the more sinister sounding 'coercive' style. The reason is that it does have an important and easily justified role to play. It works well in crises when there is little time available to adopt more inclusive styles. It can work well when the leader is an expert and the group isn't (although the leader must also pay attention to the development needs in the group – adopting the more supportive coaching style – see p.83).

The directive style may also be used when a team member is performing poorly and some of the more personal styles, such as the affiliative style (see p.81), have been tried without success.

brilliant tip

What we know for certain is that a manager who adopts the directive approach inappropriately finds it hard to make it work when it *really* needs to be used (the 'cry wolf' scenario). Sparing but appropriate use of this style delivers the result. Regular misuse means the team will cease to respond or respond in a grudging, lethargic and possibly destructive manner.

Visionary style

Teams need a vision and goals and a good leader will inspire a team to achieve them. The visionary style connects the work that the team is doing to the overall goals of the team and the organisation as a whole. People see a purpose to their work and are more motivated as a result. However, this style is more than just the creation of a vision and goals and the march to reach them. The visionary team leader monitors work and checks that the team is on course. Not only does the visionary leader make sure that the vision and goals are clear, they also make sure that everyone is 'on-side'.

brilliant tip

In some teams there is every chance that team members may know as much if not more than the team leader. In those circumstances, to use the regular articulation of vision and goals as a motivational tool may be counter-productive.

Affiliative style

The affiliative style is a closer personal style. The team leader who uses this style believes a harmonious team environment will deliver the best results. It is therefore a good style to adopt: during personal disagreements and conflicts; as the first step in dealing with poor performance (when you are perhaps taking more of a counselling role if 'personal reasons' are the cause of a performance drop within the team); or when trying to bring together a diffuse or varied group of individuals.

brilliant tip

Hay Group's research indicates that the affiliative style is best used in conjunction with some of the other styles – in particular with the visionary, participative and coaching styles. Used on its own the team leader may find that the team, while itself fostering good team relationships, is not focused sufficiently on tasks.

Participative style

Formerly known as 'democratic' this style is all about getting inputs from the team. The team leader utilising the participative style believes that commitment comes through involvement and participation. It is a good style to adopt when problem solving (non-crisis situations), for idea generation or when you, the team leader, are not sure of the best way forward. Getting input from team members assumes that you have respect for the team's competence, experience and capacity to input usefully.

brilliant tip

The leader using the participative style has to be sincere. You cannot ask for team inputs and then ignore those inputs or treat the whole thing as a cosmetic exercise.

Pacesetting style

This style is suited to the action types – sales managers or leaders in the professions who have high expectations of themselves and others. It is the classic 'leading by example' style, the assumption being that if I perform dynamically then everyone will follow. Those that do follow tend to have a high degree of self-responsibility and are likely to be as motivated to achieve as the pacesetting leader. Use this style with care.

brilliant tip

Like all the other styles the pacesetting style has a place if used appropriately. However, don't try to use this style when your team is inexperienced, has limited knowledge or lacks focus.

Coaching style

This style has been said to have the most positive impact on individuals and the team because it is about the development of team members over the medium and long term. Leaders need to build the team's capacity and the coaching style does this best. Research does however indicate that it is also one of the least used styles. These types of question should be absolutely central to any team leader's thinking:

- What can I do to increase the team's capability?
- What skills does xxx need to do her existing job better and to take on new tasks?
- What parts of my job could be done just as well by team members if they had a bit more knowledge?

If you leave the office late every night and the team seems to be underutilised, perhaps another good question to ask yourself is 'WHY?' Perhaps a bit more delegation linked with coaching and development is needed. Great teams have strong learning cultures and this goes beyond the role of the leader as the single source of new knowledge. Teams should be places where team members are encouraged to give feedback to each other (see Chapter 6) and where the team is always asking the question, 'How can we do better?' It is a question a team leader should always be asking team members too.

brilliant tip

The coaching style does not demand that the team leader does all of the developmental work themselves. It is about the way that the leader sets the tone for learning and development. It recognises that without new knowledge and skills the team withers and dies.

For you to try

If you are in a team leadership role why not look at each of these styles in turn and try to think of situations in your work where each one could work for you and situations where they might not be so useful. Think about team members and which styles they may individually prefer. For example, some may like the closer, more personal affiliative style but for others it will be a complete turn-off.

think about leaders who you have known in the past

You may have been using some of these styles anyway but hadn't attached a label to them before. Think about leaders who you have known in the past who have adopted these styles appropriately and inappropriately. What were the effects?

Three things for team leaders to consider

1 'We' not 'me'

As the designated team leader remember that when you get results as a team you share the success with the team. The language to the outside world is the language of 'we' not the language of 'me' as in 'We did it' not 'I did it'. The team will never let you lead them again if you take all the credit. And everyone else will get to hear about it too.

2 Connecting with the team

In fact, as successive generations become less deferential to those in authority, designated leaders have had to work very hard at those qualities which will enable them to earn the sobriquet 'leader'. This might come about as a result of charisma, expertise, experience, proven success and enough people believing that you have clarity of vision. One of the critical factors is that you have to connect with the worlds of those you are leading. This is why words such as empathy, trust and sincerity are now seen as core leadership traits. Of course, they probably always were.

3 A team of leaders

As the designated leader you should not fear a team with lots of leaders in it. A true test of a designated leader's confidence is when you feel able to allow someone else to take the team forward – to assume some sort of leadership role – without feeling a loss of overall authority and control.

But none of this means an abdication of responsibility from the designated leader in the eyes of those beyond the team. The designated leader cannot point the finger of blame at others if things go wrong and neither can they take all of the credit when things go well. Sounds like a bad deal? Not at all. The best team leaders can take pride in the team that gets results. The best team leaders get huge pleasure from seeing team members perform beyond a level they thought possible. The best team leaders know that a successful team reflects well on the leader without them having to tell everyone how wonderful they are.

brilliant recap

Leadership capacity in the team

- Brilliant teams require leadership throughout the team – people who can step up and take the team forward when required. If the team is a large one this is essential. We can no longer look to the one person who is the designated leader to do this.

- Teams often need to work at speed, responding to internal and external needs faster and delivering project work in shorter time-scales. Leaders stimulate this responsiveness.

- Recognise what it is that you bring to the team – when your knowledge and skills are needed you need to be ready to lead the team forward.

- Teams need to be thinking about the internal leadership capacity. Your team needs you to be ready to lead.

When you are the designated leader

Work on the application of the six leadership styles. Within these six styles we find many of the attributes required of good team leaders. So while no one will be using all of these styles, all of the time, they contain great points of reference for current and aspiring team leaders. Team leaders looking at what they can 'do' to strengthen their role in the team should consider the following:

- Directive: Give clear instructions to the team when the situation demands it.

- Visionary: Create a vision for the team and inspire the team to 'go for it'.

- Affiliative: Empathise with team members.

- Participative: Be consultative and inclusive with the team.

- Pacesetting: 'Model the way' – setting the best possible example to the team.

- Coaching: Create a team that is continually learning and improving.

This chapter has raised a key issue in team leadership – the need for the team to be motivated enough to think through and achieve team goals. As this chapter has suggested there are a number of ways that this can be done. The next chapter looks at how the team can come together to set goals for itself. However the team is led – in a more equitable, consensual environment or with a dominating leader – the result (the attainment of those goals) will be the basis for how the team is judged.

CHAPTER 5

Setting team goals

We learn from looking back. We achieve when we look forward.

In most situations the setting of team goals works best when it is a collaborative process between team members. As a team member you are then more likely to commit to a goal with both your heart and your head: the emotional *and* the rational side of us need to be won over if true commitment is to be secured. In the past 20 years many organisations have recognised the value of a more participative approach to goal setting. Whether you are a team member or a team leader there is every chance that you spend some of your time planning, prioritising and organising the team's work on a short-, medium- and long-term basis. Goal setting forms an essential part of this process. If you don't set any goals how do you measure success?

SMARTER

Management writer Peter Drucker was the first to really nail down a formula for goal setting. Many readers will be familiar with the formula although the version overleaf is an adaptation of his original. The SMART acronym suggests goals should be:

S Specific ('this is exactly what we are going to achieve')

M Measurable ('this is the measure we are using to see if we got there')

A Agreed ('commitment comes best from agreement')

R Realistic ('if it is unrealistic we are unlikely to achieve it')

T Timed ('this is when we are going to do it by').

More recently E and R have been added to make SMARTER:

E Energising ('if we aren't energised to deliver, we won't')

R Reviewed ('what can we learn, what can we do better next time?').

Drucker's model is a very logical method for developing your own tightly defined target or goal but teams should be wary of getting too hung up on getting the target absolutely right. It is more important to have a statement that everyone can feel motivated to achieve than it is to have a rigidly worked through goal/target for which no one feels any affinity.

> have a statement that everyone can feel motivated to achieve

If you can get to the tightly defined goal *and everyone feels totally committed to it* then do it. But if the team is being 'lost' in the pursuit of perfection then at least having *something* to work towards is very important, even if it isn't what might be described as perfect.

A team vision exercise – 'Here is the News'

As the exercise opposite illustrates it might actually be your higher goal – your vision of where you want to get to – which is critical.

I often begin seminars for teams setting goals for themselves by using a classic exercise, one that any team can try at any time.

Try the following:

Imagine you are a news reporting team. Pick a point in the future – one year, two years, three years. You need to prepare a five-minute news report that focuses on the success you have achieved as a team in that time. You may choose to focus on one achievement, which is symbolic of the overall success you have had, or present a more general report.

The point you pick in the future will depend on the nature of the vision you and the team are trying to create. Parameters may also need to be set to prevent the exercise becoming a fantasy one. While fantasy is fun, realism is crucial here – although it is useful to remember that one person's fantasy is just as likely to be someone else's reality so teams shouldn't set the parameters too tightly.

What is interesting is that if, say, the team comprises 10 people and you divide them into 3 groups you may get 3 substantially different reports. That in itself is no bad thing – we all have different aspirations, wishes and desires – but extreme variation may be a sign that there is some vagueness about the direction in which the team is heading.

The vision catalyst

Doing this exercise in your team can be an excellent catalyst for nailing down what it is that your team is wanting to achieve. By talking through these reports a defining vision emerges and, as a result, key goals and targets which everyone can agree and commit to are defined. This is a simple, valuable exercise. Used in conjunction with the advice given on the next few pages your team can become results driven – the point of setting goals in the first place.

Setting goals and targets

Your team is likely to have goals set for it via one of two methods – or both:

1 Your team is handed the big goals from higher up in your organisation's hierarchy.

2 The top team sets the values and vision of your organisation as a whole but you and your team mates (through the team's designated leader) translate these values and the overall vision into meaningful goals for the team.

This chapter is concerned with the second of these – where your team has a degree of autonomy in its goal setting. Teams operating via the first method may not have the freedom to choose their goals but they do have the freedom to choose how they go about achieving them. If this is the case for your team you will find it useful to read the team target triangle section at the end of this chapter (see p.102).

Goal setting the modern way

Historically, teams have often had to fight hard for a degree of autonomy. In the past 20 years things have changed. In more enlightened organisations senior management have recognised that a rigidly imposed series of goals set above the team's head, in which the team itself (team members as well as the team leader) have had little input, does not inspire the best out of people. You may well be operating in the modern way where you and team collaborators (because that is what you are here) have substantial input into the goals you set and in the way you go about achieving them.

In his great book *The Dinosaur Strain*, writer Mark Brown suggests a very interesting way of getting teams to set their own goals. Mark originally wrote this at the end of the 1980s and yet it is a system that many forward-thinking organisations are now using as a way of empowering teams and getting them more closely aligned to the overall vision and values at the top of the organisation. The thinking is that the more input a team has into its goals and *modus operandi* the more the emotional 'heart' of the team, as well as its rational 'head', will be won over.

Mark Brown illustrates the process as shown in Figure 5.1.

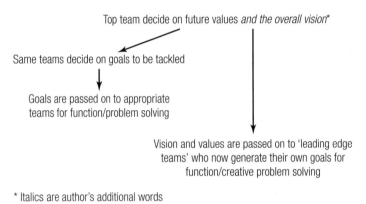

Top team decide on future values *and the overall vision**

Same teams decide on goals to be tackled

Goals are passed on to appropriate
teams for function/problem solving

Vision and values are passed on to 'leading edge
teams' who now generate their own goals for
function/creative problem solving

* Italics are author's additional words

Figure 5.1 Getting teams to set their own goals

The key here is the emphasis on vision and values. Your values have been interpreted as the way in which you check the rightness of your vision. By saying 'This is what we stand up for, this is what we believe in' your senior team defines the values within which the organisation works and, as an extension of that, the overall vision.

> the key here is the emphasis on vision and values

Your team is then free to take the vision and values espoused at senior level and develop your team goals. The ever-shifting sands on which senior management sit have created a degree of autonomy as teams are given a chance to prove themselves. The rest of this chapter devotes itself to how you and your team colleagues can create meaningful team goals.

> ⭐ **brilliant** tip
>
> In his book *The Seven Habits of Highly Effective People* the writer Steven Covey defines one of his habits as the ability to focus on the end result when you set goals – not to get absorbed in all the detail too soon:
>
> *Create a clear, mutual understanding of what needs to be accomplished, focusing on what, not how: results not methods.*
>
> His thoughts, while aimed at individuals, apply equally to teams, departments and even organisations as a whole.

10 suggestions for setting team goals

So, the team is now empowered to set its own goals. How do you go about it? The SMARTER model highlighted earlier in the chapter is a great starting off point and still hasn't been bettered 50 years after its conception. But there are many other factors to look at when considering team goals and targets, which are listed in the 10 tips below. Do not attempt to satisfy the requirements set out in all of these tips at the same time. They are guides and pointers, so use all of them *some of the time*.

1 How do we eat an elephant?

Remember the old joke, 'How do you eat an elephant?' The answer: 'In small, bite-size pieces.' Sometimes the big goal just looks too big to be possible. The answer here is to break it down to a scale that is manageable and easy to follow. Team leaders reading this need to work hard to make the vision and the big long-term goals meaningful for team members and likewise team members reading this need to ask what the big stuff really means for them in their individual team roles. The big question for anyone in a team to ask is how to make 'the elephant' a practical tool for action in the team's day-to-day work.

With the big goals it can be hard to judge how well you're doing. Timelines – deadlines for the attainment of sub-goals that help deliver the main team goal – are the team's way of checking the accuracy of its direction. Timelines are important because they tell you whether you are on track or not.

Key points

- Break the big goals up into manageable chunks.
- Use interim deadlines as a means of monitoring progress.

2 Being 'goal fixated'

Goal fixation can blind the team to the fact that the world has moved on. You may be a research and development (R&D) team working on a new product or a sales team promoting a special line. But another R&D team at another company has beaten you to the punch and got its product out there first. Customers might be sending out big signals to the sales team that they do not want the product line you are offering. You may decide not to give up in either case. But you need to pause and see if the direction you are heading is still the right one.

It is worth remembering that teams that are trying to create the perfect goal aren't actually doing anything to achieve it. Teams can quickly become inert if their debates become too centred around tightly defined goals. It regularly happens in work teams – lots of talk about what the team is trying to do, but very little action in trying to deliver. Teams who like the big philosophical discussions about direction are less good at getting stuff done.

Key points

- Remember that goal setting and goal 'doing' are not the same thing.
- Keep your head up to what is going on around you in the world.
- Be ready to move on if your goal has become redundant in the wider context.

3 What are we going to do exactly?

Is it better to say 'I want to drive a car' or to say 'I am going to pass my driving test'? Most would opt for the latter because it has a more specific deliverable. Where you can, a team should strive to be as specific as it can when it sets goals for itself – without self-paralysis!

Goals should also test the capabilities of team members because goals are best actioned where you, as a team member, feel your capabilities are being stretched (but not unrealistically).

Key points
● Beware vague goals.
● Make sure goals are testing but not unobtainable.

4 How long is success?

While what gets measured gets done some things are also beyond measure. The driving test example above said that 'Pass my driving test' is better than 'I want to drive a car'. 'I want to pass my driving test by the end of the year' is better still because it contains a measure.

But teams should be careful here. In the public sector the pursuit of government targets can be motivating for some teams and paralysing for others. In addition, the measure of 'success' is so narrow or irrelevant sometimes as to be meaningless. You can be convinced that you are succeeding because you have hit a target but the target might bear little relation to the world in which you are operating. Measures can be great drivers for the team. But they can mean focus on entirely the wrong performance area.

measures can be great drivers for the team

Key points

- Create a measure where you can that will help you define what success is.
- Don't create a measure just for the sake of doing so.
- Remember the quote attributed to nineteenth-century British prime minister Benjamin Disraeli about 'lies, damn lies and statistics'. Ask, 'Does the measure mean anything?'

5 Are we growing as a team?

As the R in SMARTER implies, your team should always be looking to review how it did in relation to its goals. This can be a valuable learning experience for the team: it gets the chance to see what it has done well and what it has done less well. The timelines in the first suggestion are also good intermediate stop-off points to enable you to do this. As individuals you should not be defensive in a team review meeting but neither should you be looking to point the finger of blame at certain individuals.

In *The Six Habits of Highly Effective Teams* writers Steven Kohn and Vincent O'Donnell give the following very sound advice when a team is reviewing performance:

It is a unique opportunity to frame all assessments – positive and negative – in terms of the team, thus reinforcing team identity and the relationships of members to the team itself.

What they are saying here is that team reviews should relate all points about performance back to the team and not individuals.

Kohn and O'Donnell also wisely point out that while reviews are often conducted close to the 'event', to do so right after it might be counter-productive if emotions are heightened. Sometimes things need to settle down again before a review.

brilliant tip

It is a common criticism of children's TV programmes that they have to have learning content in them to justify their commissioning. 'Why can't children have a bit of fun now and again?' some say. This writer agrees and it applies equally to adults too. Team working should be enjoyable even if the work is serious. Too much analysis, too much searching for 'What can we learn from this?' and the fun and enjoyment quickly gets stripped out. For all the desire for continuous learning, the team will be learning little if it isn't getting pleasure and enjoyment from its activities. Chill out sometimes. Not everything needs to be a 'learning experience'.

Key points

- Use reviews as an opportunity for the team to learn.
- Relate performance issues to the team rather than to individuals.
- Don't get so analytical that you stop enjoying yourselves.

6 Are we enjoying the 'here and now'?

In my book *Positive Thinking, Positive Action* I suggested that:

A captured moment of spontaneity can be far more rewarding than the rigidly planned pursuit of goals.

Teams that look in one direction with a fixed gaze (at the goal, for example) may find that they miss all of the other things happening around them. There could be other opportunities missed; opportunities that may only be there for a short period of time; evidence that suggests the team needs to be moving in a different direction; the spark that gets the team out of its one-dimensional rut.

▶ brilliant example

You may be one of those people who are quite happy 'living in the moment'. You could be very useful because you might be willing to try new things with no preconceived idea of where you might end up. Rigid adherence to goals can create inflexibility and narrow approaches. Life itself does not operate in a linear, structured form. Think of a sports team, struggling to get its structured game working in a match situation, who are desperate for spontaneity to kick-start it into action. Quite often it is the team member who is quite happy to operate on their wits who creates the direction that the team seeks.

Key points

- New opportunities only open themselves up if the team is prepared to see them.

- You can still be goal-focused and keep open-minded about the possibility of something new and interesting opening up before you.

- As a team member you should welcome one or two people into the team who operate spontaneously – even if this can be infuriating!

7 Is there room to play?

Suggestion 6 leads neatly on to 7 – having room to 'play' at work. There should be room within defined goals for personal experimentation and movement. There are several reasons, including the following, for this:

- Experimentation 'now' opens up opportunities in the future. Google, for example, allow 20 per cent 'playtime' for their employees – time when employees are allowed to 'play' and experiment in worlds beyond their job description and the immediate goals of the organisation. This creates the opportunities – and the new goals – of the future. Without these the team creates little future for itself.

● Everyone needs a break from the push to achieve the pre-determined goals. Taking time out to do something else that is different is refreshing and can reinvigorate you and team colleagues for the tougher battles.

Key points

● Great teams have a balance of tightly defined goals and room for creative experimentation.

● Team members should be allowed 'Google-style' playtime to open up the chance of future growth.

● A break from the pursuit of a goal can be refreshing.

8 What are we good at?

It was the great psychologist Martin Seligman who suggested that individuals work on their 'signature strengths' where the temptation is often to focus on weaknesses only. These are the strengths that define you as an individual and make you who you are. Teams have signature strengths too. Here are a few questions that your team might find it valuable to answer:

● What might observers say about your team and what it delivers?

● What do you do well?

● Is it a better use of the team's time to be nurturing its strengths or correcting its weaknesses when time is always at a premium?

● Can you pull up your weaknesses anyway if you work hard on the strengths?

● Would an overemphasis on weaknesses be demotivating for the team when it is excellent in a number of areas?

Key points

● Enjoy what it is that makes your team 'brilliant' – its signature strengths – and base your goals around those strengths.

● Address weaknesses.

● But don't address them to the point that your team generates far too much team stress by doing so.

● It might be easier to address the weaknesses by bringing in someone from outside the team.

9 Is the team in a vacuum?

Your team cannot live in a world of its own. It is likely to serve outside groups such as customers, the wider department of which the team is a part, other teams or senior management. Or perhaps all of these? In spite of all this necessary external contact it is easy for the team to cocoon itself. The team begins to look inwards rather than beyond itself and can start to lose its sense of reality if the navel-gazing becomes serious.

> your team cannot live in a world of its own

To avoid this, and to ensure that your team's goals are pitched in reality, invite people outside the team to have input when the team sets goals. By involving people outside the team you get a greater level of buy-in and support for what the team is trying to do. When you call for help – as teams often do – those with a 'stake', who feel involved in the team's work, will be more inclined to work with you through the problems (even customers).

Key points

● Keep your feet on the ground by looking 'out' rather than 'in'.

● Involve stakeholders at all stages.

● Involvement gains commitment.

10 Why the apathy?

The first chapter of this book looked at the critical role individuals such as you play in providing valuable energy to your and the team's work. Once described as the eighth deadly sin, apathy is the thing that kills off the possibility that a team might achieve its goals. In fact where apathy exists there may well not be any meaningful goal setting in the first place.

Put yourself in a senior manager's place. What would you prefer out of these two options?

1   A team that sets its own goals based on the values and vision of the organisation and delivers on them.

Or

2   A team that has to be told what its goals are by the senior team because the team is apathetic to the vision and values of the organisation as a whole.

OK, life isn't as simple as that but we can do a lot to help ourselves here.

Key points

- It is as much your responsibility to have input into discussions around team goals as it is anyone else's.
- The more you put in at the goal-setting stage, the greater identification you will feel with the work of the team as it strives to achieve its goals.
- Success breeds greater autonomy.

Team target triangle

The team now has its goals – or targets as they will be called in this next section. What next? The team target triangle is a systematic three-step process for taking a target from its conception (by following at least some of the advice in this chapter) through to successful completion. It can be used equally by team members to assess how they are likely to respond to the target once it has been set and by team leaders who want to do the same assessment for the team as a whole. It is based on the idea that the setting of targets and goals is often, as has been seen in this chapter, a systematic 'head'-based process. But the drive to work towards these targets will be dependent on a more emotional process – the connection with the 'heart'. The rest of this chapter looks at this emotion-based approach from the team's perspective.

There are three variables to look for when assessing how teams and individuals respond to the team targets once they have been set. These are motivation, attitude and energy, and can be shown like this:

Target achieved = **E**nergy + **A**ttitude + **M**otivation or simply 'TEAM' for ease of memory, where

T = Target (or goal)

Achieved through:

E = Energy (maximum)

A = Attitude (great)

M = Motivation (high)

This emphasises that the attainment of a target depends on these three factors. An illustration of how they connect is shown in the triangle in Figure 5.2 overleaf. The 'target achieved' element of this comes from energy because this is most closely associated with the action required to deliver on the target set. The interconnectivity of motivation, attitude and energy is expressed via two-way arrows because they feed off each other. Once the target has been set the team enters into a collective three-step psychological process.

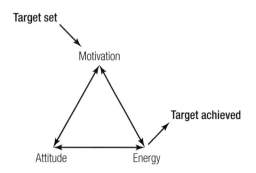

Figure 5.2 The three factors for target achievement

Motivation

Motivation makes us decide what you/the team want to do (achieve the target/goal) – 'I/We want to do this.' How much you/the team 'wants to do this' will depend on:

- identification with the overall vision and values of the organisation;
- how much of a say the team has had in the setting of the target (crucial);
- how much success the team has had already;
- how well the team is being led by the team leader; and
- whether or not team members feel the team has the capacity to achieve the target.

Attitude

Attitude makes you/the team decide how I/we do it (achieve the target/goal) – 'and this is how I/we are going to do it'.

How you/your team goes about doing this will depend on:

- how motivated the team is;
- how empowered the team feels to go out and do it;
- how aware the team is that it is always free to choose its attitude to the doing of anything; and
- the freedom your team has to interpret what the target means.

Energy

Energy makes you/the team decide how much I/we put into doing it (achieve the target/goal) – 'and this is what I/we are going to give to achieve it'.

How much energy the team puts into this will depend on:

- the collective attitude of the team;
- how many risks the team is willing to take;
- the fear of failure; and
- how long the team has been together (too long can lead to a decline in the team's energy).

What is important here is that your team's leader *and* team members should be able to talk through a number of key questions. How empowered is the team? What skills does the team have? What are the repercussions if the team makes mistakes? How much input do team members have into the setting of the target in the first place?

> how empowered is the team?

If your team is motivated, team members have great attitudes and they are full of energy in the critical action phase then there is every chance that your team will achieve the target. Success in the attainment of team targets can inspire teams to want to achieve more and hence they respond when a new target is set (see Figure 5.3 overleaf).

Figure 5.3 Setting a new target

Number 5 in our 10 suggestions recommended that team members should see themselves as part of a team that learns and grows together. Regular progress reviews should often open up opportunities for learning and development for the team as a whole. If your team is to survive then its own growth and development has to be at the forefront of its thinking. Without it there may be few opportunities for goals and targets in the future.

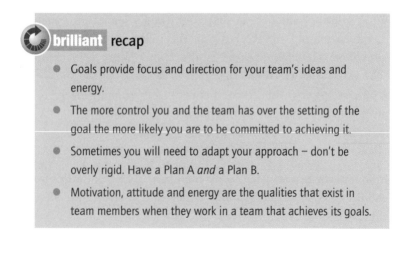

brilliant recap

- Goals provide focus and direction for your team's ideas and energy.

- The more control you and the team has over the setting of the goal the more likely you are to be committed to achieving it.

- Sometimes you will need to adapt your approach – don't be overly rigid. Have a Plan A *and* a Plan B.

- Motivation, attitude and energy are the qualities that exist in team members when they work in a team that achieves its goals.

CHAPTER 6

Team meetings and briefings

Remember that when you are in a meeting you are not actually
doing *anything. And neither is anyone else in the team.*

We all spend more and more time in meetings – your team probably meets at least once a week as a group but you probably have smaller, shorter satellite meetings on a regular basis also. Meetings at their best can be efficient, dynamic and a great way of reaching decisions that the team can commit to. Or meetings can be places where great ideas are crushed, where unhelpful displays of ego are paraded and where the team talks itself into paralysis. We've probably all experienced the best and worst kind of meetings.

There are three factors that determine the success of a meeting:

1 How the meeting is organised beforehand.

2 How the meeting is run.

3 How individuals behave in the meeting.

The first issue here is the third of these factors – how you 'perform' your role in team meetings. Later on this chapter looks at some of the more interesting approaches that you and the team can take that will enhance team performance in the meeting. Plus it gives you some tips if you are running the meeting. But let's begin with you and your role – after all, it is the only thing you can be certain of improving.

How can you be the best you can possibly be?

You have two areas to work on here:

1 Your *preparation* before the team meeting.

2 Your *performance* in the team meeting.

Your preparation before the team meeting

Many team meetings are doomed to failure because of lack of preparation. This is not just the fault of the meeting organiser who is setting the agenda or the person chairing the meeting. It is as much your responsibility as a participant to prepare for meetings as it is for the chairperson or the organiser. Team meetings are not something that just 'happen' to you.

> it is as much your responsibility as a participant to prepare for meetings

Here are some things you can do as a participant to help you play your part:

- *Review.* Read your minutes from the previous meeting. Have you acted on those things that you committed to at the previous meeting? How often do you hear the words 'I haven't had time to do it yet' as team members try to find a reason for inaction? What they often mean is that they forgot to do it or had insufficient drive to meet their commitments from the previous meeting. Maintain your own standards.

- *Agenda.* In the best teams the setting of the agenda should be a consultative exercise between team members. However, this may not always be practical. What is certain is that you should make sure you are familiar with the agenda and that you are clear what your contribution is meant to be.

- *Consider your approach.* Do you have things to say that may be sensitive? Perhaps you have some radical ideas? Think about how other team members may react to what you have to say. Try to frame what you have to say in a non-confrontational, empathic way. It may be that you have an idiosyncratic style. The team may be very used to your personal style and see it as a benefit to the team. Nonetheless don't always feel the need to perform to the crowd. Be yourself but don't be a performing seal.

Your performance in the meeting

- *Listen.* Just as you would expect to be listened to when you have something to say in a team meeting, you should make it clear to the speaker that you, at least, are listening to them. You are free to disagree but you can only disagree if you have heard what the other person has had to say.

- *Take notes.* Although properly run meetings will have minutes, it is always useful to have a personalised note of your observations, point of view, commitments and any personal actions that discussions have triggered in your mind.

- *Wholehearted commitment.* Don't commit to things to which you are not committed. They will not get done properly. If you have concerns this is your opportunity to air them.

- *Passive vs active.* The best meetings are those where the naturally passive are encouraged and the active take an inclusive approach. If you are an active team member you can help bring the quieter members of the team into team discussions. The quieter ones often have golden nuggets of insight because they spend their quiet times doing some thinking.

Being 'present'

Being in a team means being committed to a team. While great teams welcome and accommodate quirkiness, diverse personalities, off-the-wall perspectives and all kinds of difference there are some lines drawn firmly in the sand. The following is a simple checklist of meeting-damaging behaviour.

Taking phone calls/sending e-mails in meetings

Your mobile phone/portable device/laptop should be switched off – no 'digi-foraging'. It is offensive to others in the room if this is not the case. Are you at the meeting or not at the meeting?

---

brilliant example

'Being present' – Leah's story

I work for a well-known international 'agency' in one of the world's most difficult countries to operate in. Our team meetings and briefings had often had a chaotic feel. This was mainly because many people thought it acceptable to both take and receive phone calls and text messages in meetings. Most did try to hide the fact they were on the phone but a few thought it acceptable to carry on as though there was no one else in the room.

One day we had an ambassador present who was there to hear a briefing one of our team was giving on the forthcoming elections in the country. There were about 20 people present. At the beginning of the meeting the ambassador made a point of turning off his mobile phone and asked everyone to make sure that they did the same. Apparently he made a point of doing this when present at any meeting. Everyone got the message. If one of the most important people in the country could do this then so could we. Above all he signalled to the speaker that she had his undivided attention while she spoke and that what she was going to say was personally important to him.

Signalling disinterest in team members and what they have to say

'Behaviour breeds behaviour' as they say. If you signal disinterest in others (through your body language in particular) then there is no reason why they should be interested in you and what you have to say. You get the behaviour back that you deserve.

> 'behaviour breeds behaviour'

Showing lack of support for the work of other colleagues

Meetings should be places of energy, encouragement, ideas and support. A colleague airs a problem. Do you suggest ways you can help or do you let them sink in their own challenges? Someone has an interesting idea – do you welcome it? Do you assassinate the idea at the first opportunity or do you seek to build on it?

Disagreeing and *being disagreeable while you do it*

Disagreement is healthy. Meetings that become environments of continual 'nodding heads' agreement are not healthy and are often a sign that the same group of people has been working too long together. The challenge is to be agreeable whilst disagreeing. This means not interrupting when the other person is speaking (good advice at all times), truly listening and framing what you say in language that the rest of the group can relate to. It does mean being totally in control of your emotions.

Drawing attention to personal 'weaknesses'/character flaws in other team members

Everyone has weaknesses. One of the great things about the best teams is that where team members have weaknesses, others in the team will have strengths that balance out those weaknesses and vulnerabilities. Are you perfect? And would you like someone to draw attention to those imperfections in front of the group? Remember the Biblical saying:

So when they continued asking him, he lifted up himself, and said unto them, 'He that is without sin among you, let him first cast a stone at her.'

brilliant tip

There is a mantra that you can carry with you whenever you are with team colleagues in meetings. It is simply that *team time belongs to the team*. Be a fully paid-up, committed, supportive, efficient member of the team and meetings will become what they should be. You should be the best you can possibly be.

Team meetings with a difference

One of the challenges with team meetings that are held on a regular basis – weekly, for example – is to keep them fresh and vibrant. Here are some suggestions to help you and the team do this.

The 'quick' team briefing

Do you ever have those quick meetings or briefings when the team gathers together to discuss something specific? Say 10 or 15 minutes to give out some information or to air a problem and come to a quick decision? What normally happens? First, everyone has to have coffee with them (even though they've already had three cups and it's only 9.30am). Second, they like to get comfy in the chair. Third, they reacquaint themselves with colleagues by talking about what they did last night. Finally, 20 minutes later a couple of stragglers turn up. The result: the 10-minute briefing/meeting lasts for an hour or more.

brilliant timesaver

Here are some ideas for saving time in meetings:

- Ban coffee (no machine in the room).
- Remove the chairs. People don't like to stand for more than 10 minutes unless they've got alcohol in their hand, so the meeting is likely to be brisk and brief.
- Do you need a table? If it's only a place to put down the coffee, why bother?
- Start on time, no matter who isn't there. The late arrivals will soon get the message if you are walking out of the meeting room as they are entering it.

Visual stimuli

Ever seen a presentation in a team meeting where the speaker is reading off the slide word-for-word and you are reading along with them? Perhaps you yourself spend more time on your slides when preparing for a meeting than you do on what you are going to say? Remember that PowerPoint is usually a hearing aid and not a visual one because 'the audience' in the meeting is reading the slide, karaoke style, along with

> badly used slides are classic energy killers

the speaker. Badly used slides are classic energy killers in team meetings. They are mostly 'passive'. Here are some tips.

brilliant tips

- People are most stimulated when we tap into their 'VHF' channel – that is to say 'Visual, Hearing, Feeling'. We remember best when these three 'senses' are tickled – and if your meetings aren't 'memorable' then there is no point holding them.

- Consider having PowerPoint-free meetings and the opportunity for a more creative approach.

- Search imaginatively for visual stimuli (posters, different coloured drinking water for different agenda issues, etc.) to keep the meeting sparkling.

- If you are using charts with lots of numbers and figures, hang them on the wall. Team members can get up and move around, and keep their blood and oxygen circulation going.

- Use only pictures in your slides (thereby making them 'visual') or discipline yourself so that you use no more than five words. Why all the logos, borders, tables, silly MS sound effects, charts, etc.? Get rid of them. Identikit PowerPoint presentations kill the energy in the room.

- Use music to create 'mood'.

Meeting feasting

So you've had a Danish pastry, two croissants, about half a dozen boiled sweets and a few mints to keep your breath fresh after all that coffee you've drunk. One minute you're 'wired' from all the carbs and sugar. The next minute your energy levels have dropped through the floor. So you have a double strength espresso to wake you up again. And so it goes on. Everyone else in the team is doing the same thing.

Here are some tips.

brilliant tips

- Keep the food to an absolute minimum. Digestion diverts the energy needed for thinking.
- If food is necessary then provide nothing too stodgy or sweet. Schedule coffee breaks rather than have it on tap – it's a good chance for a proper break anyway (see below).
- Always have water available for meetings lasting longer than 30 minutes.

Taking a break

Those immortal words 'we've a lot to get through today, so we are not going to have a break'. Most of us struggle to concentrate for more than 45 minutes without a break, a change of pace or physical movement. And we don't all have a football-sized bladder either.

✖ brilliant dos and don'ts

Do

✔ Build in 5–7 minute breaks every 45–50 minutes but be disciplined about returning on time. Very few people are able to sustain concentration for more than an hour at a time.

✔ Brief someone outside the team (or a team member who is not required at the meeting) to come and get participants if they are urgently required elsewhere.

✔ Use energisers (www.businessballs.com is a great source of these) to keep life in the room at 'low' points.

✔ Avoid the three-hour meeting unless absolutely necessary and don't make a regular habit of it.

Don't

✖ Use the break to go and check e-mails, make phone calls, etc. You cannot deal with anything properly in that short period of time so why start?

✖ Ignore some of the more wacky ideas to energise meetings. Some American organisations use short bursts of physical exercise/movement to keep energy levels high. Don't laugh at the idea... why not try it?

Leaving the meeting

Ten people in the room. Only four of them with any interest in the agenda issue under discussion. The others, including you, sit round thinking of the other things you could be doing. Does this happen to you? Not just in your own team meetings but in meetings generally?

Note: When I raise this issue in workshops on meetings many participants reply that it is not acceptable in their organisation to leave meetings before the end. I sense that sometimes this is a convenient excuse for not trying rather than the reality. I suspect that many will be impressed that you, at least, are seen to be in control of your own time if you make a point of leaving a meeting once your agenda issues have been covered. If the cultural issue is true then I raise the following as key points for the team.

brilliant timesaver

- Make it culturally acceptable for people to leave meetings when there are agenda issues being discussed that do not concern them.

- Make it culturally acceptable in the team that team members can ask the 'How long do you need me in the meeting for?' question to the person organising the agenda (you do have agendas don't you?).

- Remember how much it costs your organisation to have people in unnecessary meetings. Here is bit of elementary maths to help you do this:

  How many hours do you spend in meetings per week when you do not need to be there – 3 perhaps? Then multiply that figure 3 by the amount of money it costs your employer to employ you per hour (£20 x 3?). Then multiply that figure (£60) by 48 (the number of weeks per year you are at work). Then write down the number (£2,880). That's the amount of money it costs your employer to have you in meetings you do not need to be at per year. That could be your pay rise (or your manager's).

  If you really want to hammer the message home, multiply that figure by the number of employees in your organisation – for example, the calculation based on an organisation of 500 people is as follows:

500	x	2,880	=	£1,440,000
No. of employees	x	Waste per employee p.a.	=	Waste p.a.

  Now that's a lot of money.

brilliant tip

Sometimes teams have a meeting because that's what the team does once a week. Do you sometimes have meetings because routine dictates it? Perhaps the equation above will convince you that wasting time in unnecessary meetings can cost you your pay rise. And the pay rises of everyone else in the team too.

Better team meetings

Agenda

When I run seminars on meetings everyone says that the first thing you do is to create an agenda. And yet, when I ask how many meetings have the discipline of an agenda most say 'sometimes'. A disappointingly high number confess 'never'. Any meeting that has two or more issues under discussion needs an agenda and a time allocation for each agenda issue.

Allocating time

Time on agenda issues should be allocated on the basis of importance. Time is also a function of priority. Although priority issues may not be important ones the deadline on less-important issues may dictate that they need to be allocated time for discussion in a meeting. The key here is to be brutal about the time allocated. It is all too easy for a team to drift into a one-hour discussion about staggering lunch breaks when there are far more important issues to be discussed.

Ego exercise

Meetings are not arenas in which certain individuals get the chance to exercise their ego to a wider audience. Meetings should be places where everyone has the chance to say what they think – honestly and openly – but where the rights of team mates are respected through the use of appropriate behaviour. Seek the participation of all team members. The quieter ones often have nuggets of insight that take the team's thinking forward – but do they get the chance to express them?

Share roles

If you have a regular team meeting (say once a week), alternate the roles. Who does the logistics, sets and circulates the agenda, keeps time, chairs it? It is a great way of helping the team to understand how important these issues are to brilliant team meetings and it also widens the skills base of the team.

The minutes of all meetings should also be taken. Most people can't remember what they did three days ago let alone what they talked about. Meeting minutes provide an essential *aide-mémoire* for you – what was discussed in bullet point form and what each member of the team – including you – agreed to act on.

Team decisions

Too much 'hard-thinking'

Decisions are often made after a rigorous analysis of hard facts. But decision making is just as much about gut feeling. In individuals this is often expressed as intuition. In teams it may be a collective feeling that a particular course of action is the right one and one that the team can commit to. But beware that it feels right because the decision is 'safe' or a rehash of what you have been doing before. You should feel a real energy, perhaps even a passion, about the decision and the actions that the decision involves.

brilliant recap

- Prepare properly for a meeting – read the agenda and the minutes from the last team meeting, and prepare your overall approach and expected contribution.

- 'Be present' at all times in a meeting – phone off, full attention on other speakers, a collaborative rather than confrontational approach with team colleagues.

- Meetings should be well organised, as brief as possible, interesting and imaginative.

- Think about the waste associated with poorly-run team meetings.

- Keep thinking about ways your team meetings can be run better – agendas, participative culture, decisive environment.

Meetings are great places for observing the relationships that exist between team members. Body language, choice of words and the level of listening and questioning all give strong clues as to the strengths of relationships within the team. The strength of these relationships will also help the team in its decision making. Many teams will make decisions in group forums such as team meetings, but they will do so in a way that lacks vitality and, more importantly, will often take the easiest, most comfortable decision rather than the right one.

In the next chapter we will look at tools, tips and techniques that will add focus, dynamism and energy to your decision making. And, of course, help you to make better decisions.

CHAPTER 7

Teams and decision making

Meetings are places where great ideas are discussed and quietly strangled.

Winston Fletcher

Most decisions are taken by groups of people but, as Winston Fletcher's comment implies, it is easy for decision making to become an orgy of idea bashing – an obsessive search for the reasons why certain ideas won't work – rather than an exploration of possibility. What is needed is balance. The gathering of appropriate information to help inform the decision-making process and an awareness of risk (which need not itself be a barrier as long as the team is aware of the risk) need to be offset with a good dose of emotional connection to the decision taken.

In this chapter we look at the six key stages in team decision making:

1 What is the problem?
2 Information gathering.
3 Idea generation.
4 Evaluating ideas.
5 Making the decision.
6 Implementation.

In stages four, five and six we look more closely at some of the factors – both environmental and practical – within a team that help or hinder effective decision making, and also look at some key tools to help you make the best decisions with your colleagues. Many of the elements involved in stages one, two and three are covered in more detail in Chapter 10.

The key stages

Stage one – what is the problem?

It is important that teams have been through a number of crucial steps before decisions are taken. Decisions usually need to be made for one of two reasons:

1 There is a problem to be solved.
2 There is an opportunity to do something better or different.

It is unfortunate that working life often seems to be little more than a series of problem-solving activities and the emphasis therefore in this chapter will be on team problem solving. However, a more progressive team should also be looking out for opportunities – exploiting weaknesses in competitors (sporting or business); a chance to improve; an opening in the market.

First, we need an accurate definition of what the problem is. For example, you might think that the problem you are trying to solve is 'How can we communicate better?' But the real problem might be 'How can we reduce the amount of e-mail we send?' Some groups spend too much time addressing symptoms or subsidiary problems rather than the root cause of the problem.

> we need an accurate definition of what the problem is

So, stage one is to ask: *'What is the problem?'* (Or opportunity!) This creates a goal for your team – solve the problem or develop the opportunity – not forgetting the fact that problems can also be great opportunities.

brilliant tip

Groups start to come up with problem-solving ideas (often jumping at the first one) before they have nailed down what the problem is – what has become known as 'premature articulation'. Don't start generating problem-solving ideas too soon.

Stage two – information gathering

In stage two, teams need to gather information that will both help you to generate ideas (stage three) and also provide data that can be helpful when your team starts to evaluate the options available.

brilliant tip

Information gathering is important. Information overload is a hindrance. If we need complete information to justify any decision we might take we will never have enough. So, don't use excessive information gathering as an excuse not to take the decisions the team needs to take in a later stage.

Stage three – idea generation

Chapter 10 provides extensive advice on idea generation in groups – what has become known as 'brainstorming'. A second, increasingly popular variation on this – 'Post-it note brainstorming' – is also included.

Groups are often prey to linear, one-dimensional thinking in this idea development stage, offering up ideas that have been relentlessly discussed already, are already being used or just have a very 'safe' feel about them. This is also a weakness with teams that have been around for a long time in that they work from an ever-dwindling number of 'safe' ideas. In the early stages of team development, teams are often dynamic and innovative but, over time, inertia and lack of engagement, and therefore insight, kick in with the result that teams produce less ideas than they did previously.

While these one-dimensional ideas are a very important part of the idea generation stage, your team should always strive to think multi-dimensionally, looking for ideas that create evolutionary or even revolutionary change.

brilliant tip

Don't be put off by the apparent wackiness of playful, multi-dimensional thinking – wild, crazy ideas may appear.

Stage four – evaluating ideas

This stage is undertaken with a cool rational head – sifting through all of the available information that supports (or not) all the possible options identified in stage three. There are a number of techniques available to help us do this but the first question to ask is: 'How critical is the decision?'

How much time on the decision?

It is not unusual to see groups spending hours discussing minor issues and not giving the time to issues and problems which need cool rational discussion and debate. Analysis needs to be controlled during all the stages by asking: 'Is the analysis – and the time spent on this analysis – justified by the importance/priority of the decision?' Decisions do need to be taken on minor issues like scheduling lunch breaks and who parks where in the car park, but these should not be taking up time that could be used on priority/important decisions.

> analysis needs to be controlled during all the stages

Focusing on irrelevancies

Identified in the previous chapter as a classic meeting timewaster, this is also a killer in decision making. Often minor points or complete irrelevancies are used as justification for slowing up or halting the decision-making process. As has been said often in this book, asking the 'Does this get us nearer our goal?' type question sharpens up the team's thinking and keeps the team focused on the matter at hand.

Who is saying what?

One of your primary information sources will be people, both in the team and beyond it. It's easy to listen to the loud, opinionated types but your team needs to be careful who it listens to. We have 'experts' at work whose motivation will be to give you the information you need to help your team make the best decision. However, we all know the 'experts' who are self-seeking, selective in the information they give or keen to create inertia (or all three!). They are likely to be looking at decisions from their perspective rather than yours.

> your team needs to be careful who it listens to

> ### brilliant tip
>
> Try to avoid information bias when evaluating options. For example, on a personal level Apple Mac users are noted for their deep, emotional attachment to their machines, but while you might want to ask a Mac user's advice when weighing up a PC- or Mac-buying option, you should look for specifics rather than emotive arguments to help you in your buying decision. This writer has both and might be the best person to talk to!

Everybody has an opinion but the team should be careful to prioritise the information provided by informed and rational thinkers.

And finally at this stage, here are two excellent idea 'elimination' techniques that make decision making less complex.

1 Clustering

Clustering is useful where your team has a large number of ideas from the idea generation stage and it is trying to make sense of them. Putting them into clusters or groups may make it easier to eliminate, or move forward with, certain groups of ideas. Clustering is also useful as it can help identify similarities across ideas that at first sight don't seem to be connected.

Clustering may not identify the best solution but it does get you nearer to finding it.

2 *What* must *we have?*

in decision making it is easy to be side-tracked by irrelevancies

In decision making it is easy to be side-tracked by irrelevancies or luxuries, particularly when your team is presented with a number of options. In this situation a refocus on what you *must* have rather than what you would *like* to have – essentials rather than luxuries – will prevent straying. The brilliant example below shows how this can work in practice.

This method works well when your criteria are clear and when you want to shut emotional contamination out of decision making. Teams are prone to talk themselves into things when they should sometimes be talking themselves out of them! This method can also work well when ideas are generated over a long period of time, which seems to be increasingly happening on intranets where organisations are encouraging the modern-day version of the suggestion box.

'Musts' may typically include budgetary factors; people and how they will be affected by your team's decision (often the most unpredictable element in decision making); risk factors such as customers and the unpredictability of your market; and organisational cultures and how receptive they are to your team's problem-solving ideas.

brilliant example

Imagine that your team comprises of a group of regional sales managers who are deciding what the new company car should be for your sales reps. You are discussing what the car needs to have, i.e. assessing the buying criteria. And, of course, you have a budget so you can't have everything you want. You therefore place your criteria into three groups:

1   Things we *must* have.

2   Things we *want* to have.

3   Things we would *like* to have.

The team then looks at all the features of the potential cars on offer:

- Price (a *must*, i.e. it cannot exceed budget).
- Fuel economy (possibly a *must*).
- 1600cc or bigger engine (*must* or *want* depending on volume of mileage).

▷

- GPS (probably a *must* these days).

- MP3 docking station (could be *must*, *want* or *like* depending on circumstances).

- 0–60 in 5 seconds (a *like!*).

And the list of criteria may go on.

Two experts in problem solving and decision making, Kepner and Tregoe, have taken this process one step further and I have adapted their system. Here, a scoring system is used in which all possibilities are taken and filtered through the 'musts, wants, likes' stages, eliminating possibilities as you go. In our example above, all of the cars need to get through the 'must' stage and score a maximum 10 points if they do so. Failure to score 10 means elimination.

In a more subjective second stage, marks out of 10 are given for meeting the 'want' criteria. If the car under consideration meets all of the criteria it scores 10, and that maximum score is reduced where some of the '*want*' criteria are not met. Where scores are still equal a third elimination stage – 'like' – can be used to determine a winner or 'winners'. After all, the team concerned could give the option of two cars to its sales reps.

You may find that these evaluation techniques reveal the best solution to your team. This makes stage five – making the decision – so much easier (though not necessarily 'easy'). What we know is critical in both stages – indeed in all the stages – is the behaviour of individuals. While Chapter 10 looks at behaviour in idea generation/creative thinking, there are rules of behaviour around decision making too. In particular the need for effective non-prejudicial, non-judgemental questioning and, linked to this, the importance of listening.

If you or a team member feels that you are not being listened to, friction between you and colleagues may result. And if you don't listen to others, you will be basing your own opinions on faulty thinking because you will not have all the facts (because you haven't been listening!).

Stage five – making the decision

You are now honing the many ideas that you and your team mates hopefully have and are closer to the point where you can make a decision. Here are some suggestions to help you do this better. We start with the softer but highly important element in decision making, intuition.

Intuition

Decisions are often made after a rigorous analysis of hard facts. But decision making is just as much about gut feeling. In individuals this is often expressed as intuition. In teams it may be a collective feeling that a particular course of action is the right one and one that the team can commit to. But beware the feeling that it feels right because the decision is 'safe' or a rehash of what you have been doing before. You should feel a real energy, perhaps even a passion, about the decision and the actions that the decision involves. In my sister book to this one, *Brilliant Idea*, I identified three elements connected to team/group intuition and how it can work for you and your team:

> decision making is just as much about gut feeling

1 *Needs*: Do we need to make a decision at all?

2 *Awareness*: Assuming we do need to make a decision, it is important that we feel deeply about the outcome.

3 *Belief*: Heightened connectivity to the outcome of a problem-solving exercise allows us to tune into a higher realm of personal and collective performance.

Of course, this softer process needs to be balanced by practical, easy-to-follow methods too.

Voting

The voting approach can work well when you need simply to get a majority commitment to a solution or idea when debate has been going on too long, or to clarify where you are at when the differences are small. This is important because, although you may have minor objections to a solution, these objections may be procedural or administrative and do not mean that you are against the solution *per se*.

However, it is important that voting does not leave resentment among team members who feel that their ideas and objections have not been examined properly.

Why perfection?

It can be tempting to feel that there is one true perfect solution – the cognitive solution – that we strive for. While in some circumstances this may be true, trying to predict sales for the next year and basing stockholding on that decision will ultimately prove to be true or not. However, in many situations the need to make a decision will transcend the need for it to be the perfect decision. Eighty per cent rather than 100 per cent right will do just fine. In those situations there is no need to agonise over the right decision. You may just need to toss a coin!

Paralysis often comes about because teams are worried about making the 'wrong' decision and talk through issues to the nth degree. While key issues should never be left underdiscussed, absorption with minutiae can paralyse (perhaps through fear) the team's capacity to make a decision. This is not an excuse to cut corners in gathering the necessary information to help make the right decision, but we must recognise that passion and energy provide the necessary propulsion when the decision is implemented. With no passion any decision taken is irrelevant.

Beware conformity pressure

There are a number of reasons why people seek to conform to the group's thinking and it can be damaging to the team if conformity pressure becomes too strong. The reasons include the following:

- Some of us feel intimidated by the more voluble members of the team.
- A lack of confidence in expressing our own views.
- Some of us need time to think things through.
- Laziness – it is easier just to go with the flow.

Team leaders reading this book must encourage the reticent, be prepared to silence the voluble and give time, where possible, for decisions to be debated properly. But this isn't just a team leader's responsibility. It is the responsibility of all team members to be as open and democratic as possible for as long as possible. Collective decision making needs collective input and without it we don't get commitment.

> be as open and democratic as possible for as long as possible

brilliant tip

So, you have agreement? Fearful of conformity pressure or hasty decision making? A possible antidote when you fear that the team has reached agreement too soon or without proper debate is to state the agreed solution and then ask that over the next week, before the team meets again, team members raise objections and counter-arguments. The solution will become more robust if it has been subject to the rigour of counter-argument and debate, with the team being given a little extra time to think it through. This is also an excellent way of making sure that emotional contamination doesn't occur – the group being overly excited by a 'shiny' jewel of an idea without thinking it through properly.

Stage six – implementation

Implementation requires a balance between the head and the heart. Without clear, cool, rational thinking decision making is compromised. Without commitment to the decision – an emotional *feeling* that it is the right decision (or the best available in the circumstances) – the team will not be motivated to deliver.

Your team needs to consider three factors in implementation.

1 Attitude

Without positive attitude and commitment from all members of the team any decision taken is immediately compromised. There is a need for balance between heart and head, but do not underestimate heart because it propels our decision forward into the outside world.

2 Influence and persuasion

Although idea implementation has been thought through, teams often miss out the need to influence others to take on board the team's decision. A number of strategies are available to the team to demonstrate that the decision is a good one:

- *Evidence*: What supports the decision?
- *Consequence*: What happens if you don't act?
- *Reward*: What are the benefits?
- *Direction*: What will the result be?
- *Trust*: People will tend to be persuaded by the group's decision if your team has invested time in developing relationships with others.

brilliant tip

While these influencing strategies are very useful at this stage, your team may like to consider using them in earlier stages of the decision-making process. The earlier people are involved, the more likely they are to be committed to the decision that your team takes.

3 Culture

Your team needs to give consideration to the type of culture it operates in. Just as every country has its defining cultures and subcultures, all collections of people – whether they be multinational companies, local councils and authorities or sports teams – do so as well.

Decision implementation requires four questions to be asked when establishing cultural type:

1 Are we operating in an environment with a strong central power source (perhaps even one person)? If so we will need to consider how to influence the source best, with 'consequence', 'reward' and 'direction' the most likely to bring success. Means may be less important.

2 Are we operating in a highly bureaucratic, hierarchical culture? If so we will need to make sure that we are following procedure and that we have used clear systematic thinking. We must also make sure that we haven't gone above people's heads in the hierarchy. Means and method mean a lot.

3 Are we operating in a culture that is very task and results based? If so we will need to emphasise results and the 'direction' strategy may be best here.

4 Are we operating in a culture with one driven personality? Although all of the influencing/persuasion strategies are available here we may need to think about strength numbers. Can we enlist the support of other teams in getting our decisions implemented?

brilliant tip

The team has to be open to making adjustments if circumstances change or if certain elements of the decision were not quite right. The flexibility required in earlier stages is just as important in this final implementation stage. Just because a decision has been made and implemented does not mean that the team rigidly adheres to it. Ask what needs to be changed, adapted or moulded.

brilliant recap

- Decisions are made because we either have a problem to solve or have an opportunity to develop. Sometimes these are the same thing.

- Be clear what the problem is. Causes not symptoms.

- Gather as much information as you can to aid your decision making but not so much that you paralyse the team's judgemental faculty.

- Teams should utilise 'multi-dimensional thinking' in idea generation. The wild and the routine should happily coexist.

- Give the appropriate amount of time to make decisions. Where it is possible, important decisions require time and team debate.

- A good balance between the head (the rational, logical) and the heart (the emotional, inspirational) is valuable in decision making.

- Follow the six-stage process.

Good decision making in teams highlights the need for two contradictory elements – the need for unity while at the same time encouraging individualistic thinking. Your personal behaviour, whether you are the team leader or a team member, will play an important part in creating unity. We are willing to adopt the 'all-for-one, one-for-all' mentality if we feel we have been involved fully in the decision-making process and that our ideas have been listened to. As in so many elements of human behaviour, try to be to others as you would like others to be to you. Harmony rather than discord is more likely to result even when there has been disagreement.

Teams often find themselves making decisions under considerable pressure. In fact, the best teams often only show themselves at their best when there is this pressure. In the next chapter we will look at pressure from the team perspective and this includes a section on decision making when pressure threatens to incapacitate a team's critical thinking.

Note: Readers who wish to read more about team decision making should have a look at my sister book to this one, *Brilliant Idea*. Chapters 6, 7 and 8 are particularly relevant.

CHAPTER 8

Teams under pressure

...laughter is a social activity – and the evidence is vast that people who have regular, satisfying connections to other people are healthier and happier.

Daniel Pink, *A Whole New Mind*

The first thing I notice when a team is under too much pressure is that it ceases to be any fun to work in. There is no joy, no laughter. The second is that while the team might be working hard, its output is misdirected or disjointed. In the worst cases there is little discernable output. This short chapter aims to help teams avoid some of the pitfalls when working under pressure. But first a key question – what exactly is 'pressure'?

brilliant definitions

We need to differentiate between two kinds of pressure. 'Positive pressure' enables a team to perform at, or beyond, the sum of its constituent parts. Of course, as with individuals the amount of pressure teams can take varies from group to group.

'Negative pressure' means that the collective effort of the group fails to reach the accumulated effort of its constituent parts – the team members.

Writers on stress and pressure Eve Warren and Caroline Toll suggest that there are some universal factors that create 'pressure points'. These are the factors which, if teams and individuals aren't aware of them (and, of course, don't respond to), can adversely affect the welfare of the team. Pressure points for your team may include:

● Tight deadlines.

● Conflict between team members.

● Problem avoidance/weak decision making.

● Lack of clearly defined roles.

● Underperforming team members or team members not taking responsibility.

● Poor leadership/coordination.

● Not enough real listening.

Many of the interpersonal factors are explored in other chapters, e.g. poor relationships, lack of personal responsibility, weak decision making, ineffectual leadership. This chapter therefore aims to highlight some of the task-fulfilment challenges that teams have when working under pressure and how to overcome them. These are:

● Conformist thinking.

● Task completion obsession.

● Loss of perspective.

● Focusing on the negative.

● Easy excuses.

Conformist thinking

Under pressure it is easy to close off views that are controversial. Pressure creates a bunker mentality which makes it difficult to absorb anything outside a very narrow band of conformity.

It may be that just at the moment when we need to strike out in a new way, take a risk or rethink the way we are solving a problem, we revert to predictable thinking.

It is important to recognise the difference between situations where pressure is created by the need for an immediate response – which may require a 'set' or predetermined way of solving the problem – and situations where pressure is not crisis-led or a 'yesterday-driven' deadline. In these situations new ideas may be needed (see Chapter 10).

Task completion obsession

Pressure can make us think both individually and collectively 'Let's just get the task done' and move on without consideration of ways and means. Or, as with the conformist thinking above, the desire to get the task done results in a lack of ideas – we focus on the immediate. Pressure can also heighten sensitivity to criticism. That means we avoid actions that could be liable to criticism in the future – we play safe.

> pressure can also heighten sensitivity to criticism

As a team be aware of the following:

- Getting the task done rather than 'done right' can mean lack of attention to detail. In haste elementary mistakes are made. So make sure the detail people (nearly every team has them) are not ignored.

- The team needs to develop a tough skin. Criticism should be expected and heard. No one ever got through a tough situation by not taking a (well thought through) risk or two, and where there is a risk there is likely to be a critic.

- Pressure getting too much? It sounds obvious but why not try to reduce the pressure? The pressure may be as much about the way you work under pressure as it is the work itself. The desire for immediate task completion creates its own tension and our rational, clear thinking can be compromised. The team will benefit from taking a step back and learning to:

1 Plan better.

2 Respond to a realistic rather than an unnecessarily tight deadline.

- Teams performing well can and should have disagreements, but these disagreements should focus on the *task* and how it can be performed better and not on personal and personality issues. Don't keep pointing the finger of blame at miscreants. Disagreements within the team can too easily be turned into personality issues.

- Embrace ambiguity. Pressure can decrease the tolerance the team has for ambiguity. The desire to complete the task overrides (wrongly) the necessity to navigate through choppy waters. Learn to embrace ambiguity and to understand that while a black and white world is easy to navigate, more often it is the shades of grey that have to be understood. This takes time.

Loss of perspective

Work is a part of life but it is not life itself. When under pressure, we individually and collectively risk seeing our world as the centre of the universe with everything else revolving around it. The importance of what we do becomes exaggerated in the wider scheme of things.

> work is a part of life but it is not life itself

This creates an additional and unnecessary pressure out of all proportion to the original source of the pressure and makes us less able to respond. In the worst cases the team becomes paralysed through misplaced 'fear'.

Remember to keep the challenges the team faces in perspective. As an individual make sure you have a 'hinterland' – hobbies, interests and activities that show another side of life to you and take you away from the pressure the team is under.

brilliant tip

Keep your sense of humour and fun intact. As the author Daniel Pink says, 'laughter means not thinking' and this can help take team members away from pressure for a while. Remember to socialise together – to enjoy each other's company away from workplace pressures. Morale can drop when under threat and it is essential that team members are able to enjoy each other's company in situations other than high-pressured ones. Your colleagues may become associated solely with pain rather than pleasure otherwise.

Focusing on the negative

It is easy to slip into negative conversation at the best of times – how often, for example, do team meetings feel like endless problem-solving discussions? When under pressure it often seems that the only things that are happening to the team are bad, and conversations – both individually and collectively – seem to focus on things which aren't working. While we shouldn't shy away from problem solving we also need to balance that with reminders to ourselves about the positive aspects of the team. Questions such as those below can help:

- What makes this team good – what do we do well?
- What success have we had?
- What do we like about working in this team?

brilliant tip

A good way to keep the team thinking positively is to remember the value of acknowledgement. We all like to feel valued so specific and justified praise and thanks are primary motivators in life, and are great for maintaining a positive working environment in the team.

Easy excuses

At the time of writing it looks as though the global economic challenges which presented themselves in 2007–08 may be with us up to 2015–16 and perhaps beyond. Some people are using this to justify some of the most self-seeking behaviour imaginable. People ask themselves if they shouldn't just be looking after themselves – doing everything they can to secure their job even if this means that others are affected. Certainly it pays to develop personal survival strategies but one of those strategies should be to work with people, not against them or in competition with them.

This book has mentioned many people who have reached stratospheric levels of success – sports stars, musicians, business people and so on. They have two things in common. The first is that they have all succeeded when under a great deal of pressure. The second is that all of them have said how they could not have succeeded without a great team around them. The lesson here is that even if your agenda is a personal one, you won't achieve it without the help of your colleagues. If it is good enough for those who are operating under a degree of pressure that many of us will never experience, it must be a sensible strategy for the rest of us.

Maintain good interpersonal relationships and be prepared to put in the extra effort to strengthen these when under additional pressure.

brilliant tip

Think about how you personally have behaved when you have felt under pressure outside the workplace. You probably needed some sort of security. The comfort of your family and friends or perhaps visiting a place which has sentimental resonance. Teams are no different. When under pressure it is the strength of relationships within the team that provides the collective resolve necessary to overcome challenges. Work on your relationships – it is probably the single most important thing you can do beyond applying the knowledge and skills that brought you to the team in the first place.

brilliant dos and don'ts

Here are some dos and don'ts that also work as a recap for this chapter:

Do

✔ Identify the 'pressure points' for your own team. Some will be universal, others will be unique to your circumstances.

✔ Work to realistic deadlines unless a crisis situation demands an immediate response.

✔ Keep a sense of humour – it's not THAT important.

✔ Remember what's good about the team and the people in it.

✔ Work hard to preserve good relationships in the team when times are tough.

Don't

✘ Stifle creativity.

✘ Be task-obsessed to the exclusion of idea generation.

✘ Assume that your team's world is THE world. Keep perspective.

✘ Use self-preservation as an excuse for bad behaviour.

In the next chapter we look at 10 classic team traps. You will find that the advice contained within a number of these identified traps, e.g. '10 Poor communication', will also serve the team well when working under pressure.

The 10 classic
team traps

There's nothing wrong with failure if it catalyses the team to get it right next time.

In my introduction to this book I suggested that having a team of great people does not guarantee success. There are many reasons why some teams fail and others succeed and it goes beyond who is in the team. You of course are great – or you aspire to being so – but is your team? While this book concentrates on what can make you successful, studies also show some common themes among teams that fail. These traps are the ones that slowly evolve without you really noticing. They are subtle and frequently found alongside teams who have been together for a long time. New teams start with the best of intentions – focused on the job, results driven, meetings full of focus, energy and ideas (and conflict too) – but over time we can lose the critical thinking that keeps the team on its toes.

> new teams start with the best of intentions

brilliant example

Many readers will remember the classic piece in the Monty Python film *The Life of Brian*, where the People's Front of Judea (PFJ) have lost sight of what they are trying to do (overthrow the Roman occupation) and are discussing

PFJ member Stan's right to have babies. If you haven't seen the clip of the film the 'References and acknowledgements' section of this book directs you to the YouTube clip of it.

As you watch the piece you get the impression that the PFJ have been together rather a long time. They have become part of the fabric of the Roman Empire (no more than a minor itch to 'the oppressor') when they were originally conceived as a party that was going to destroy the Romans. They have lost their direction, too wrapped up in ideological purity and internal politics to be able to be a dynamic fighting force. They have almost given up on their goal. Politically-minded UK readers will recall the Labour party of the 1980s and the Conservative party of the 1990s doing a similar thing. Other readers will no doubt have their own examples from their own political environment.

OK, maybe I shouldn't be analysing something so deeply that was just meant to be funny but the PFJ shows some of the classic symptoms of a team in real trouble – loss of sense of priority; focus on irrelevancies; the search for ideological perfection; single-issue obsessions.

These and other symptoms – 10 in total – are examined in this chapter together with suggested cures. You will notice that some of the cures appear more than once.

1 What are we here for?

The symptoms

The possible symptoms include:

- Lots of misdirected energy. In other words, plenty of effort but a lack of real achievement.
- Lack of understanding of why the team exists in the first place – 'What are we actually trying to achieve?'

- When you yourself are unclear how your own goals contribute to the overall goals of the team.
- Few, or poorly set, goals/targets.

The cure – what's important?

Teams do not exist for their own sake – they have to have a point for their existence. It might be an R&D team at a pharmaceutical company researching a cure for cancer or musicians recording a new album. Perhaps a rugby team analysing it's game plan or a newly formed charity working in Russian orphanages planning its *modus operandi*. Remind yourselves regularly what it is you are setting out to achieve. The advice on goal/target setting in Chapter 5 will be useful but here we are also talking about the value of the team's vision. This might be expressed as a team mission statement.

A key question to ask is: 'Does what we are doing/discussing get us closer to achieving what we exist to do?' It's the question to ask regularly if you feel the team is losing direction. How does this help us in the team's work? Does it make a contribution or is it irrelevant? This is also an excellent aid in creative problem solving and decision making (see Chapters 7 and 10). The solutions suggested might be highly creative (or indeed not) but do they actually solve the problems that are preventing us from achieving our goals?

2 Our world is THE world

The symptoms

The symptoms include:

- Teams building up walls around themselves with their own systems, procedures and limited view. The *raison d'être* becomes introspection and, as a result, the team gets isolated.

- The methods become more important than the end result.

- An overemphasis on internal irrelevancies. Sometimes this might be the endless pursuit of perfection (the PFJ's pursuit of ideological perfection in our earlier example) to the detriment of the team's need for action.

- The 'silo' phenomenon that business writers and thinkers talk so much about is evident. (This occurs when different groups of people – teams or departments, for example – start to operate in isolated 'silos' which have little or no contact with other teams or deparments and often the wider world.)

- Distrust of senior management. The team protects itself by cutting lines of communication between itself and senior management, further distancing itself from the world outside.

The cure – make the connection

Teams do not live in sealed boxes. Their purpose will relate to activity that affects people beyond the team. How you connect internal dynamism with external orientation will be the variable between success and failure. In other parts of this chapter advice is offered on how to reconnect with the worlds beyond the team.

> teams do not live in sealed boxes

The opposite can happen where teams are very good at updating their mental models of the worlds in which they operate but less good at telling others. Sales teams, for example, often have high-quality market information on tap because of their front-line exposure and yet the competitor information does not feed back. Perhaps this is in part due to the pace good sales teams operate at, in that they progress from one sale to the next without pause for breath.

brilliant tip

Teams always need a 'face'. Someone – or hopefully more than 'one' – who keeps the team connected to the outside. These people perform your essential market research role – helping the team to keep up to date with the worlds of those it serves and perhaps too the worlds of the future. Can you formally assign this role?

3 Single-issue obsessions

The symptoms

Are you letting one person's obsession (or your obsession) become the obsession of the team too? The example featured earlier from *The Life of Brian* had in its origins one of the PFJ members, Stan, wanting to be a woman. Fine, of course, but irrelevant to the PFJ and what it was trying to do. Having great ideas and trying to get them enacted is one thing. Taking the team off on a tangent for the benefit of a personal agenda is not helpful.

The cure – does it help us deliver?

A balance needs to be struck between the need for ideas and initiatives that help the team deliver on its goals and the wilful exploration of pet projects and obsessions that take the team off on unnecessary tangents. Always refocus on what the team is aiming to achieve and ask the '*Does it help us achieve this?*' type questions.

4 Reality distortion

The symptoms

If you look under the same stone you are only likely to see the same things. And those 'things' may well not be a mirror to what is happening in the real world. How in touch with reality is the team? How many other stones are you turning over?

A second symptom here might be only seeing things that you want to see. It might be inconvenient to see reality, so as a team we shut out the possibility of contrary evidence.

The cure – look under other stones

This cure is a recognition that there is life beyond the team and its internal dynamics. We become introspective when we isolate ourselves and we start to believe that there is nothing else out there to look at.

Teams should also work through a range of options in decision making to avoid what is known as 'selective seeing' – only using evidence that supports our view of the world and ignoring anything that doesn't.

Networkers are very useful because not only do they sell the work of the team to the outside world, but they should also be a valuable information conduit back to the team – identifying and turning over other metaphorical 'stones'.

5 Increasing bureaucracy

The symptoms

Teams working together for a period of time are inclined to add layers of procedure and policy in response to one-off problems – the team focuses on adding to the bureaucratic machine rather than reducing the size of it. It probably explains why governments, for example, seem to become more bureaucratic the longer they are in power. It is seen as a way of justifying their existence.

The cure – just do it better

Investigation often uncovers the lack of application of existing policy rather than a need for more procedures, directives and missives. But it's often easier to add to what you do rather than just doing what you do, properly. Keep it 'lean'. Can you do what you do now better? Do you just need to apply yourselves more?

6 A lack of new stimuli

The symptoms

The longer a group of people work together without the stimuli of new, fresh thinking the more the team members start to think like each other. Some even say we start to look like each other! As a result we get an ever-dwindling number of ideas, poor decision making and half-hearted action.

> team members start to think like each other

The cure – invitations

Regularly invite people from outside the team to contribute to team meetings. Step one will be people from other teams and departments where your work connects you. Step two might be to ask people from your organisation with whom the team has little contact but who can offer challenging perspectives. Step three is to invite people from outside the organisation: clients/ customers (even if your team isn't customer-facing), suppliers and those who have knowledge about the work you do but may offer a fresh viewpoint.

This is also a great generic cure for isolationism: ask for feedback on the team's work.

brilliant tip

Consultants can cost a lot of money. And yet you have a whole host of people who could give valuable insights into the work you do. These 'free consultants' are all of those people – internal and

▶

external – who have an interest in the work you do. If you see these people in a positive way rather than as a threat they can provide a great 'free of charge' stimulus to the team. That's priceless!

7 We all agree with each other

The symptoms

This is closely connected with the last symptom. Here, not enough constructive disagreement and rigorous debate lead to team stagnation and increased isolationism. The team struggles to keep up with the world out there because it doesn't allow contrary views into team debates. The team feels safe in its cocoon but doesn't realise it is slowly dying. We agree with each other and, worse than that, we believe we are right.

The cure – fresh thinking

Encourage the 'contented discontents'. The 'contented discontents' are the people who enjoy the company of the team and the team environment but are ready to challenge convention. They certainly don't want to leave the team. Often seen as an irritant ('there's Roger sounding off again'), they can be easily ignored because what they say might involve a bit of effort or because they are challenging us to get off the comfy team sofa. Is the team listening?

If you are leading the team or have a say in the appointing of new recruits look for people who are more than clones of existing team members. Like attracts like and it can be easy to recruit people who are just like us. If you want to inject fresh thinking into the team go for those who are different.

8 Resourcefulness

The symptoms

This may seem a strange one to include here because great teams should always have a degree of resourcefulness. The challenge is that a regular recourse to resourcefulness may be symptomatic of a team that is always using a sticking plaster to deal, as they see it, with the problem rather than looking at the reasons why the problem occurred in the first place.

The cure – macro-thinking

The sticking plaster problem-solving approach may be symptomatic of 'micro-thinking' – in other words, thinking small rather than looking at the bigger picture. Macro-thinking can help us ask the bigger questions – 'Why hasn't this gone well?', 'What might be causing the problem in the first place?'

9 The sepia photo

The symptoms

Teams exist to do things for others – customers, colleagues, other teams or departments. Professional sports teams are paid entertainers and the spectator has a view about what constitutes entertainment. An R&D team in the pharmaceutical industry is creating a drug for a market not for its own intellectual curiosity. An administrative team provides a service, perhaps invoicing clients or processing job applications. What

> is the team up to date on new trends?

they all have in common is that they serve others. To do this teams need to have a mental photograph of what it is they need to do to serve their stakeholders best. However, the mental snapshot captures a moment in time and indeed the camera can lie. Is the team up to date on new trends?

The leap from old world to new can happen alarmingly quickly and the team that has failed to see trends, emerging competitors and better ways to do things can quickly become irrelevant.

The cure – keep up to date

Using the mental equivalent of Photoshop – a piece of software used by graphic designers to improve images and photographs – teams need to constantly reassess the world beyond the team. If you see these people as your customers it may well be that the customers' needs, wants and desires change and your team has to change and adapt to reflect those changed circumstances. The 'Mental Photoshop' is a tool that lets you change the photo you have of the outside world – but that photo needs to be an accurate one.

10 Poor communication

The symptoms

The symptoms may be similar to those associated with some of the other team traps in this chapter. These may include:

- The team stops communicating or relies on poorly utilised communication methods such as e-mail.
- The team stops getting into the customer's world through regular contact.
- Little intrapreneurial activity beyond the team ('Intrapreneurs' are the employed version of entrepreneurs.)
- A loss of confidence in the work of the team – are you seeing your work as insignificant or unimportant?

The cure – team travel

'Team travel' means psychological travel as well as physical travel. It means getting into the worlds of those whom the team serves *and*, as a means of doing this, getting off our backsides and going to talk to those people. (Please note: e-mail is not 'talking'.)

With lack of communication (or the misuse of communication tools such as e-mail), often highlighted as the major problem in interdepartmental strife, what better way to travel to the worlds of others than talking to them?

A service team, for example, needs to get its internal workings in order but only from the customer's perspective. The key question to ask, when considering the internal processes, procedures and dynamics, is: 'Is what we are doing internally adding value to what we do in the eyes of the customer?'

Involve others, stakeholders in particular, in the work the team does.

brilliant tip

Start championing the work your team does. If you don't see value in what you do, no one else will either. Many teams in organsiations have 'open days' – lunch provided of course – where others in the organisation can get to see the work the team does and have an opportunity to give some feedback.

brilliant recap

The 10 traps in this chapter fall into three broad categories:

1   Losing a sense of priority/perspective.

2   Isolationism.

3   Siege mentality.

The three positive mindsets that can help us shake off the shackles of the three big traps are:

1   *What's important?* – to help us prioritise what it is we are meant to be doing.

2   *Team travel* – by asking if we are sufficiently close to the worlds of those the team serves.

3   *Prison breakout* (a useful catch-all phrase that covers the positive mindset that is needed to overcome a number of these traps) – to help us get out of the paralysing self-reflection that is the lot of many teams who have been together for a long time.

If you and your team colleagues can make these shackle-breaking mindsets a sort of mantra that the team repeats to itself regularly, you will go a long way to avoiding the traps that teams can fall into without really realising it.

These three overarching factors will serve teams well in almost any situation. However, we know that many teams operate in special circumstances and a number of other factors – perhaps unique to them – will also come into play.

The final chapters of this book (in Part 2: Brilliant team types) take many of the messages covered already in this book and give some additional advice to help these more specialised team types make the most of the work they are doing. However, the advice given should not just be seen as useful for specialist teams. These team types are creative teams, project teams and remote teams (where team members are diffuse), and all readers will find that their team will need to be creative, will need to perform 'one-off' pieces of work (the project) and have team members scattered during the lifecycle of the team. These are chapters that should be of interest to any team member or team leader.

PART 2

Brilliant team types

CHAPTER 10

Creative and problem-solving teams

You can't teach an old dogma new tricks.

Dorothy Parker

Western economies are at a watershed. Our companies have realised the importance of shipping process-based work where it can be done cheaper to retain competitive advantage. The public sector does the same to make its budgets stretch further. Much of this work is work that can be done without the need for deep, insightful thought. So what are we likely to be left with? Educationist and creativity writer Mark Brown suggests three factors. First, knowledge and intelligence, built up over many years will be critical although this can also be a barrier to progress when the knowledge comes in the form of too much applied 'institutional memory'. In other words, when your team or organisation says 'this is the way we do it/have always done it' then this becomes 'the way we will always do it'.

Knowledge without energy and commitment will be ultimately pointless so a real feel and connection for and with your work is the second factor, with words like 'passion' and 'engagement' helping to apply all that knowledge and intelligence to the wider world. Now we come to the third factor – and the purpose of this section – innovation and creativity. As you work out ways of doing what you do now, cheaper, perhaps the critical thing that will ensure your team's survival will be your unending capacity to innovate.

All teams need to think creatively. For some teams, such as those who form R&D departments, creative thinking as a team will be a central element in the portfolio of tools you will need to be successful. For other teams, such as those whose core function is administration, you will not need to think creatively all the time but you will fail to survive if you do not think creatively at certain, critical moments. This chapter will help your team think more creatively as a group if you operate in either of these environments.

> all teams need to think creatively

Teams need to think creatively to solve problems or to identify/make the most of opportunities. This, therefore, is the reason that in this chapter the problem or opportunity goal is often cited – '*What is the problem or opportunity for which we are generating solutions?*'

Team brainstorming – where to start?

Although brainstorming has come in for a lot of criticism, with some even suggesting that it doesn't work at all, it seems that the key problem is that idea generation in groups – what has become known as 'brainstorming' – is poorly done. Recent insights and research (see the References and acknowledgements section) show two key reasons for this:

1   In an effort to create some truly 'out there'/crazy ideas, the team is asked an 'out there'/crazy but possibly abstract question and is then told 'there is no such thing as a bad idea... yet'. Most people do not respond well when there are no parameters set on the question – we don't like vagueness or uncertainty. A small minority may respond well and end up dominating the brainstorming session but most people will end up confused and make little contribution.

2   The team is asked to generate creative ideas around existing
    knowledge and data. The result here is likely to be ideas that
    merely tinker with existing methods of operation because
    the parameters set are narrow and restrictive. The ideas
    generated are unlikely to be real breakthrough ones.

Brainstorming always begins with the team being asked a
specific question that it is then invited to grapple with. The
team tries to play a form of psychological judo with the
question itself. The key here is to ask a middle-ground question
that prevents people getting lost in vagueness and uncertainty
or being overly constrained by operating within what is already
known and routine. This doesn't restrict your team to really
going to the edge of its collective imagination. It is more that
the start point encourages inclusivity so that if the team travels
to the edge of its creative capability it does so together. This
process is explored in the next section.

A five-step process for team idea generation

Step one – ask the right question

This, as was seen in the last section, can be a 'middle-ground'
question. Writer and thinker on innovation and creativity Kevin
Coyne, along with his research team, has suggested 21 question
types to help teams ask these types of question. Perhaps one of
the best generic ones – for teams trying to overcome the common
problem of improving service standards – is the following:

*What is the biggest hassle about using or buying our product or
service that people unnecessarily tolerate without knowing it?*

At first you might think that this question is only of relevance
to, for example, a customer service team. In other words, not
relevant to the work you do. But think about this a bit more.
Imagine you are a team processing invoice payments or an

ICT department. You are of course serving others – individuals, teams and departments. And as such you should always be looking to simplify/improve your interactions with those you serve. Your team may well deliver some very interesting insights and, as a result, breakthrough thinking about service if you ask the right kind of questions.

Imagine a wider, vaguer question had been asked – such as 'How can we improve our service levels?' – with the invitation to come up with an infinite number of crazy ideas and the rider that, at this stage, all ideas are good ideas (one of the 'rules' of traditional brainstorming). It is unlikely that your team will respond as well as it did to the first question.

Step two – gestation

Educational psychologist Guy Claxton and others have suggested that many of us do not perform at our best when forced into a corner to think. He champions what he calls 'the slow way of knowing'. Think about the situations where you have your best ideas and insights. These often happen when you are not 'hard-thinking' a problem but rather when you have the problem on your mind, but it is more likely than not bubbling on the back-burner. What we might call 'soft-thinking' the problem. It's why you have those 'eureka' moments that seem to jump into your head when you are in the shower or walking in the country. Your brain is working on the problem even if you are not particularly conscious of it doing so.

For this reason, idea generation in teams may work better if teams are given the problem or opportunity question for which great ideas are needed in advance of the brainstorming session. It gives everyone a chance to put the question on the back-burner – your

your brain is slow cooking the problem

brain is slow cooking the problem or opportunity but is under little pressure to do so. When you and your team convene for the session you might find that your contribution (and the contribution of others) is stronger at the outset.

Step three – avoid domination

As a sponsor
It may well be that you are the 'sponsor' of the brainstorming session either as the team's leader/manager or because you have identified the problem or opportunity goal. In this situation it is important that you do not assume a position of power in the team. Avoid the following:

- Leading or chairing the meeting – others are likely to defer to you too easily and therefore not give the best of themselves.
- Beginning the brainstorming session with a download of your own ideas. This can easily prejudice or contaminate the thinking of others.

As the chair of the meeting
If you are chairing the brainstorming session then some of the advice in Chapter 6 on meetings will be useful here, but do remember the following:

- Suppress your own role so that you are predominantly a co-ordinator of the views of the group – getting contributions from everyone, encouraging the quiet and controlling (but not suppressing) the dominators.
- Act as a catalyst for the team discussion when ideas are drying up. You should come to the meeting prepared but should suppress your involvement once you have asked the catalysing question. A good catalyst, if the group is reaching a dead end, is to ask the team to imagine they are a group of people from a very different discipline to your own and how they would view the problem/opportunity/goal from that group's perspective.

Another useful catalyst is to ask 'what if?' type questions as in: 'What if we had to process customer invoices in two days instead of the current seven days. How might we go about it?'

As a participant

- Avoid 'yes... but' type statements. These usually take the form of 'Yes, I like the idea but we can't do it because marketing won't like it', or 'Yes, that's an interesting idea but we tried that a couple of years ago and I don't see that you will do any better now.' The result is that others feel that their ideas are being shot down in flames with you the principal assassin. They become disinclined to contribute again.

- Avoid brainstorming becoming 'blamestorming'. This occurs when you and your team mates meet to solve a pressing problem but instead indulge, by pointing the accusatory finger, in trying to blame others for the reason things have gone wrong. Looking at the reasons why things have gone wrong will often point to ways in which they can or should be done better. But this does not mean that the meeting should become personalised. Great sports coach Clive Woodward was known to deal with personal shortcomings one on one in private, but preserved the sanctity of task-based rather than individual-focused team meetings.

brilliant tip

Idea generation is not a competitive sport. Too often brainstorming sessions can become displays of ego where 'competitors' look to outdo each other with the wackiness of their ideas. The idea generator basks in an 'aren't I brilliant for being able to think like this?' glow. In the meantime other, possibly very good, ideas remain underdiscussed or undeveloped.

Step four – idea building

Ideas are great playthings. Learning to wrestle playfully with each other's ideas – without killing them off – can give impetus and energy to ideas which at first may seem to have weaknesses. There are two approaches that you can usefully take here:

1 Piggy-back ideas.

2 Ask 'What's good about it?'

Piggy-backing★

In 'piggy-backing' ideas team members build on each other's ideas. The initial idea acts as a catalyst for the thinking of others in the team. Teams who are working in this way will say things like *'That's an interesting idea, what if we…' or 'I haven't thought of it that way, we could…'* It is important that this does not become an exercise in outdoing each other. You should be idea collaborators.

What's good about it?

In team idea generation it is very tempting to dismiss ideas because there seems to be something in the idea which won't work. Although your team may be disciplining itself not to be idea-critical in the crucial idea generation phase, in their minds a number of people in your team are probably dismissing the idea because of its perceived weaknesses. These weaknesses do not mean that the idea should be dismissed. There may be a small percentage of the

> weaknesses do not mean that the idea should be dismissed

idea which is weak – say 10 or 20 per cent – but 80 per cent of the idea remains strong. The idea gets dismissed for the sake of

---

★Non-UK readers will want to know what piggy-backing is. It is a game played in schools in the UK where pairs of school children race each other. The second child jumps on the back of the first child, holding on tightly (with the first child holding the other child's thighs) and they race other pairs to the finish line.

the 10 or 20 per cent rather than championed and developed on the basis of the brilliant 80 per cent. Try to ask 'what's good about it?' when presented with new insights and ideas. The brilliant tip below suggests a way of doing this.

brilliant tip

Many writers on creative thinking at work, including Tudor Rickards and Mark Brown, have suggested using a 'yes, but... and' approach to developing the ideas of others in the team. Instead of 'yes, butting' which, as was explained earlier, can kill off the willingness of others to contribute, 'yes but... anding' allows teams to progress ideas which may have flaws but where the inherent thinking is sound or even 'brilliant'. An example of how this works might be:

*Yes, it's a great idea **but** finance may raise strong objections. If we can get finance involved early **and** make them feel part of the process rather than a necessary evil, the idea could work really well.*

brilliant example

Larry Brilliant – the value of volume

Google.org is Google's philanthropic division established by social entrepreneur Larry Brilliant. With a part of profits being allocated by Google to this endeavour the google.org team had to ask, 'To whom do we allocate these resources?'

This is the point where idea volume indicates engagement with the question. Brilliant and his team compiled a list of over 1,000 ideas from which the team took 11 to be progressed before they settled on the final 5.

This sheer volume of ideas is critical for any creative team. But it is dependent on two factors.

1 Job/idea engagement

Only when teams engage with a problem can they generate the volume of ideas required to arrive at the one or two great ones. With philanthropic causes, a highly emotive subject, engagement probably comes easily. But with less than thrilling subjects – improving administrative processes, for example – you as an individual and your team as a whole may have to work harder to truly connect with your subject.

2 Beware the dwindling idea base

A brilliant or breakthrough idea will often come only when teams strive for a volume of ideas. Beware the creative team operating from a dwindling idea base – or in the worst case from only one or two ideas. This often happens when a team has been together for a long time and where overfamiliarity with each other creates its own kind of inertia. Larry Brilliant and his google.org team had to have the 1,000 ideas initially to settle on the 5 great ones.

Brilliant himself acknowledges the value of asking the 'right question' not just in idea generation but also when selecting the best ideas. In Google's case:

How will our work help the poorest and weakest of the world?

This question came about because research has indicated that the majority of philanthropic giving does not go to the people who need it most.

Step five – meet and meet again

There are a number of reasons why teams should not limit idea generation to one session:

- Some will value the opportunity to think about ideas away from the relative hothouse of the team meeting. Some people just don't come up with their best ideas in groups and need time away to think.

- It takes away the pressure to reach a decision in the meeting itself. Team members – perhaps you yourself – operate at different speeds. This of course applies where a decision does not need to be reached at the meeting.

- Time away will give you and other team members time to accumulate information, data, other opinions, etc. to support or to help progress ideas or to make good decisions on the ideas that your team is working with.

- Meeting again signals that this is not a cosmetic exercise. One-off brainstorming sessions can be frustrating because they rarely lead anywhere. Commitment comes when team members see the session as part of a valuable process rather than an end in itself. In other words, the team becomes motivated to contribute when it feels a collective purpose in its actions.

Post-it note brainstorming

This is a fairly recent technique to help group brainstorming. Early reports (including this writer's own experience) indicate that it is a method that works well for many groups, with some suggesting they prefer it to the more traditional methods of brainstorming. It is also very useful in engaging those who typically tend to keep quite quiet during team discussions. As many readers will recognise, it is often the quieter, reflective people who have some of the most interesting ideas.

To start with we follow the same initial steps as in traditional brainstorming: 'Step one – ask the right question' (p. 171) and 'Step two – gestation' (p. 172). However, we then deviate.

Step three – use Post-it notes

Having had a period of time to reflect on the problem or opportunity for which ideas are being generated (perhaps a week if this is possible), the group comes back together. Each person is given a handful of Post-it notes and the group is provided with a whiteboard (if available) or a flipchart on which they can stick their Post-it notes. Acting independently, i.e. without discussion, each person then starts to write their ideas down on Post-it notes and places them (each time they have an idea ready) on the whiteboard. At this stage, the facilitator/ co-ordinator should observe the ideas being generated but remain silent. This is important for three reasons:

1   One of the recurring problems with traditional brainstorming is regular contamination of the group's thinking by facilitators/co-ordinators who can't help offering their own opinions or trying to steer the group's thinking in certain directions. This can be avoided, for at least a period of time, by the group 'performing' without influence from other team members or the facilitator.

2   Ideas don't get shouted down by the more vociferous team members because, at this stage, the group is still silent.

3   This way we get the valuable input of team members who don't enjoy the more open group session. This is often hard for the more extrovert members of the team to understand but it is important that they do.

Step four – cluster ideas

The next step, as a team, is to start clustering your ideas into groups. This not only helps in further idea generation (see step five overleaf), it also aids decision making later (see also Chapter 7) – certain clusters of ideas can be eradicated while others can be taken forward. This is important where there may be many, many ideas.

One of the clusters is likely to consist of the more wacky, off-the-wall ideas which cannot be easily categorised. The danger here is that this 'cluster' gets left behind or that the opposite occurs and only the left-field ideas get entertained during further discussion (see step five).

Step five – round two

Step five means a further round of idea generation. Here the facilitator can get involved but as an encourager – perhaps by calling out fresh ideas as they emerge on the whiteboard/ flipchart. The 'clusters' may help focus thinking into certain areas as the team moves towards decision making – 'Which of these ideas can we use?'

The team members who are traditionally quiet are likely to be encouraged by this process because they see their ideas being included, whereas in traditional brainstorming they are shouted down by the team, or perhaps ideas, though thought, are not even offered by the quieter person for team consideration. Thus they are inclined to generate more ideas if their ideas are not instantly shot down.

Teams can run a number of rounds of this, and as highlighted in step four teams should also look seriously at the cluster of left-field ideas for further expansion and development.

Your hyper-creative team

The following is aimed at teams for whom creative problem solving and opportunity spotting are central to their work team. The suggestions come from a number of examples – Sony, Google and IBM primarily, but others too.

Team composition

Try to incorporate people from different departments. Marketing and customer service people may add valuable conduits to the outside world if your team is in danger of operating in a creative bubble.

What kind of breakthrough is the team looking for?

There are many kinds of ideas. Your team needs to be clear on what sort of breakthrough it is looking for. Is it merely a rubber-stamping exercise for what you do already – a reminder to do what you do now, just better? Are you looking for something a little bit more creative but which isn't going to fundamentally change what you do? Or perhaps an idea that is a true shift away from the norms and conventions of your sector?

The likelihood is that in a great idea-generation session you will get ideas of all kinds. But if, say, you are looking for something truly different select the team on the basis of those who you and the team know will add some real left-field thoughts.

> in a great idea-generation session you will get ideas of all kinds

If you want to learn from other industry sectors or other departments in your own organisation and how they deal with particular problems, it makes sense to co-opt from them even if it is on a very temporary basis.

Small is beautiful

Creative teams should be small. The larger the team the greater the barrier to effective intra-team communication. Quieter voices may also struggle to get heard. If your team is a large one – say more than 8–10 – you should break up into smaller groups so that all voices get heard.

Success or failure

Innovation and creativity are experimental processes. In any experimentation there will be unknowns – things that cannot be predicted because there is no precedent. This means that mistakes will be made. Mistakes are a necessary part of creative experimentation, but make sure that you don't make the same mistake twice. Remember the old maxim:

Good judgement comes from experience. Experience comes from bad judgement.

Variety

Try to have more than one project or innovation running at any one time where possible. This avoids having everything invested in one idea. Instead you allow the best ideas and innovations to emerge.

brilliant tip

If ever a catalyst was needed to thinking creatively, why don't you and your team mates ask the 'one improvement per day' question favoured historically by Japanese businesses? In many Japanese companies the idea of 'continuous improvement' has been a living part of organisational culture since the 1960s. As part of this process teams ask themselves every day to think of one improvement to the product they offer or the service they deliver. Not all of these improvements get adopted but it's a great way to continually innovate.

brilliant recap

- All teams *must* be able to be creative. Some need to be creative more often than others.
- We need to be creative to solve a problem or to create or maximise an opportunity.

- Ask the right initial question when brainstorming ideas.
- The best creative teams spark off each other rather than seeing idea generation as a competitive sport.
- Recognise the 'value of volume' of ideas.
- Creative teams should seek a wide spectrum of views and perspectives to keep connected to the wider world and prevent introspection.

If process and procedure are being shipped out wherever they can be done cheapest (the 'outsourcing' process many readers will be familiar with), what are we left with? Even if your team thinks it exists solely to implement existing processes and procedures you and your team need to recognise that you are unlikely to survive unless you ask how things can be done better, cheaper, faster or differently.

Many organisations have set specialist project teams to do this. You will find it useful now to go on to the next chapter on project teams, particularly if your team spends much of its time creating new products or services, or innovating around existing ones.

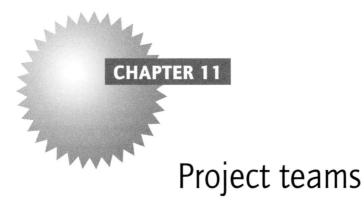

CHAPTER 11

Project teams

To the optimist, the glass is half full. To the pessimist, the glass is half empty. To the project manager, the glass is twice as big as it needs to be.

D r Chris Stringer is an expert in human evolution and the author of the seminal book *Homo Britannicus* that traces the history of the *homo* or 'man' genus in Britain going back over 700,000 years (including *homo sapiens*). The book itself condenses much brilliant research on the subject over the past 200 years, in particular the work of the up to 30-person project team he has directed since 2001, the Ancient Human Occupation of Britain project (AHOB).

With a team that varies in size between 14 and 30 depending on the nature of the current work involved Dr Stringer has a big job on his hands. In the conclusion to his book he looks at some of the issues involved in bringing a team of highly-intelligent, talented individuals together (palaeontologists, geologists, etc.) to form a brilliant research team doing some fascinating work that is influencing research in Britain and all over the world. He chronicles some of the challenges:

- *I have to make sure that the project keeps an eye on its goals and that people don't become too distracted and head down research avenues that might not be so productive or would **lead us away from our core objectives**.*

- *Sometimes, if we're putting a paper together, it can be a real challenge to find a **consensus view** to which everyone is happy to put his or her names.*

- *The whole team meets four times a year to discuss the achievements and plans for the future, and we also have workshops to discuss the future. With such a large group **opinions often vary tremendously**.*

Project team managers and team members everywhere will identify with these challenges – particularly those in bold – and can probably add many more of their own. This chapter explores some of the challenges. It is not a chapter that runs through the mechanics and technicalities of project management – a sister book to this one, *Brilliant Project Management* by Stephen Barker and Rob Cole, does this admirably. Rather it gives short, sharp tips and hints for the delivery of a successful project from the team member and team leader's perspectives.

> **this chapter gives short, sharp tips and hints**

brilliant definition

Project team

A project team is a team that undertakes a specific, definable, one-off piece of work within a specific time frame where activities need to run in a planned-for sequence. Resources are likely to be limited. The project team has a specific objective that takes people beyond their day-to-day roles.

The work of the project team can be divided into five key stages:

1 Setting up/initiation of the project.

2 Defining the project.

3 Planning the project.

4 Delivering the project.

5 Reviewing the project.

As a project team member you may be invited to join the project team during stage one or two. What is clear is that whenever you become a part of the team the attitude and energy you and fellow team members bring to the team will be a key determinant in the project's success or failure. You can make the project team leader's life easy or difficult. Try to put yourself in their shoes and always ask how you can make their job easier. Below you will find 10 additional recommendations to consider if you work in a project team or a team that has some of the characteristics of a project team, e.g. delivering a 'one-off' piece of work.

Ten recommendations for project team members

1 The project team goal

Do you know why your project team was set up in the first place? Can you express the goal or goals of the project specifically? The goal, as was seen in Chapter 5, is critical because without it all actions merely pass time rather than having a clear purpose.

You should also be clear on what is particularly important to external stakeholders, i.e. anyone outside the team who has an interest in the work of the project team.

2 Reporting

While you will report to the team leader in a formal sense, both the project team leader and other project team members will need you to be aware of the information they require from you and when. The project will depend on you hitting deadlines in order that the work of the project team can progress. Those deadlines should be agreed between you and other team members.

3 Your role

The project team will only reach its overarching goal if you and other project team members are clear on what your roles are in achieving that goal. The role is likely to be very tightly defined – unlike the greater fluidity you might have in a regular job role – and subject to specific deadlines which must be met in order that the project moves forward.

You need to be absolutely clear on the roles of the other project team members. Also, be clear about and have respect for the expertise they bring to the team.

4 Commitment to the team

The level of commitment you give to the work of your project team will be one of the variables in project success or failure. Make yourself available for progress meetings, reviews, reports from other project team members and occasional inconvenient demands. This will present a challenge when the demands of your regular job role (if you have one) mean time pressures and conflicts. We all know, however, that time is a function of priority and the team will quickly know if the project has ceased to be a priority for you.

5 Responsiveness

This is an extension to number 4, commitment. This is about your attitude to feedback from team colleagues and from people beyond the project team. It is also about responding positively to suggestions, ideas and queries others might have. It is too easy, and often unproductive, to go on the defensive. You always have the right to disagree with ideas and suggestions but you must explore the reasons why you disagree and not dismiss out of hand what was said to you with the best of intentions.

> respond positively to suggestions, ideas and queries

brilliant example

Jason's story – responding to others

I was part of a project team that was putting a new IT system in place that our call centre staff were to use. We quickly recognised that it would be a mistake just to tell the call centre team what new system they would be having. We didn't know the exact nature of the work they did and what they would be looking for the new system to do. For that reason the project became an iterative process. We liaised continuously with the call centre team, coming back to them regularly with new versions of the proposed system until they got exactly what they wanted. It sounds logical but my experience is that, particularly in IT, assumptions are made about what the end-user wants without enough consultation.

Of course it was frustrating. You spend quite a few hours tweaking software and the feedback is not what you want to hear. Or someone in the call centre team made a suggestion that, while reasonable enough, added a degree of complexity to what we were doing.

The point is that the project existed for the benefit of the call centre team, not us and it was up to us to respond to their needs.

6 'Creep'

Project creep, where the project team starts to work beyond its original definition, is one of the classic traps that project teams can fall into. If you personally feel the need to move beyond the scope of the project – perhaps because some new and interesting insights or information have come to light – you must liaise with the rest of the project team before moving ahead. There must be very good reasons to move beyond the initial definition and scope of the project. The project sponsor will also need to be consulted.

7 Team relationships

Here are five tips to help maintain strong relationships within the project team (they provide a useful reminder of much that was said in Chapter 2):

- Work on your empathy skills – understand the 'worlds' of others in the team better. Remember that others see the world differently from you and may well see the work of the team differently too.
- As has been said elsewhere in this book, constructive disagreement is great – but do it without being disagreeable.
- Really listen to other people's point of view.
- Use questioning as a tool to increase your and the team's knowledge and to understand other team members better.
- Recognise that your project team colleagues are likely to have been brought in because they have specialist knowledge and skills and should therefore command your respect.

8 Getting help

Not many people, particularly it is said more intelligent people, like to admit that they lack knowledge, are wrong or are struggling for whatever reason with a particular task. There will always be 'events' that occur that you cannot plan for which will not be your fault but for which you require help to resolve. But it is crucial to flag up problems as early as possible – don't hide them.

Just as you would welcome help and support in challenging times, be prepared to offer help and support to others when they need you.

This goes one step further. Jonathan Ive – responsible for Product Development at Apple – says this about his team:

One of the marks of the team is the sense I think of looking to be wrong.

It takes a real parking of your ego to do this but is wonderful for the development of the team and its work if you can.

9 Team blend

Open a newspaper, turn to the recruitment section and look at the recruitment ads. Sometimes they look like 'clones' of each other in that they ask for a raft of similar skills. One of the most frequent is 'good team player'. It's often hard to know what that means, but the recruiter often implicitly wants someone 'who will fit in'. Very rarely do they say 'someone who can challenge what we do', 'ask the difficult questions', 'be a little "edgy"', 'think differently', 'come up with crazy ideas', 'be an irritant', or even 'someone who finds it difficult to fit in'.

As in all other kinds of team the point is that every project team needs one or two people who are fundamentally unlike the rest of the team. They keep the team on the tips of its toes. Learn to welcome them.

> every project team needs one or two people who are fundamentally unlike the rest

10 Your language

Observe a great team – project team or not – and observe how team members refer to themselves in relation to the rest of the team. In poor teams, team members refer to 'me' when there are minor successes – reflecting any glory on to themselves. In great teams the language is always 'we'.

The lifecycle of a project – from initiation to review – will contain highs and lows for the team. As a team member you have a responsibility to keep your own energy levels up, and by being supportive and encouraging of others you can do the same for them too. Use positive language. Raise the team 'spirit level'.

A checklist for the project team leader

Although these points are aimed at the project team leader because they have the ultimate responsibility for the project, every project team member should have a full knowledge of how to define, plan and deliver a successful project. This is important for all project team members. A wide knowledge base within the team makes the project team leader's job so much easier because everyone recognises what's important. Many of the points in this checklist are good practice in many types of team – not just specially set-up project teams. Your regular team may well do 'one-off' pieces of work quite often even though it may not call itself a project team as such.

Note: As this is a book about teams in general rather than project teams the section below contains just a brief outline for both project team leader and project team members to follow. If you want to take the chance to develop your knowledge of projects, the References and acknowledgements section contains information for further reading. The section also contains various document references which are starred(*). These can be obtained easily and free of charge from many websites. For example, www.businessballs.com (scroll down the left-hand menu until you get to the 'project management skills and techniques' section). You can also use Microsoft Office Project templates.

Stage one – project initiation

Why are we doing this?
Be clear on the business case:

● Ask what contribution the project makes to the growth of the business. If this is unclear then don't do it.

● Make sure the project makes a contribution to the goals of the team, department or even the organisation as a whole.

The 'sign-off'

- Do an initial think-through of likely risk. Doing this now – making sponsors aware of the risks – prevents ugly comebacks later.

- Get finance people involved if there are significant financial implications. They can kill off your project quickly if they only come in at a later stage.

- Make sure you have clear agreement and sign-off from the sponsor of the project and appropriate senior management if necessary.

Remember:

- Review progress so far and monitor risk on an ongoing basis.

- You cannot communicate enough.

Stage two – defining the project

Clear aims

- These are defined in a project initiation document or PID* for short.

- A project can only have one driver and you need to be clear whether this is quality, costs or time.

- As well as identifying what is in the project, be clear what isn't. This helps prevent project 'creep' later on.

Roles and relationships

- Make sure everyone is aware of why they have been invited to join the project team. Do they bring a specialism to the team? This will make sure everyone is clear about the role they are expected to perform. It is important to plan for a good blend of skills and experience that reflect the work of the project. Are there any shortfalls here which need to be taken into account and which may add to the risk involved?

- Although project teams (like all other teams) work best when hierarchies are minimised, everyone needs to be clear on the reporting structure and levels of authority that they have.
- Develop a relationships map★ that identifies relationships within the team; between the team and stakeholders and between individuals and stakeholders.
- Bring all interested parties together as early as possible – many of the issues raised in the project definition stage do not have to be answered solely with the inputs of the project manager. Participants should include the project team members, the sponsor and stakeholders or stakeholders' representatives if there are too many.

Remember:

- Review progress so far and monitor risk on an ongoing basis.
- You cannot communicate enough.

Stage three – planning the project

What are we doing?

- Break the project down into all of its constituent parts. This work breakdown structure or WBS★ needs to list all of the activities associated with the project.
- Try to get these activities organised into groups and estimate how long they are likely to take.
- Develop the critical path.★ This is a chart that identifies the critical activities in the project from the beginning right through to the end, with the deadlines that need to be hit if the project is to be delivered on time. There will be many activities that cannot be performed unless the critical activities have been completed. For example, you cannot pour boiling water from a kettle into a tea cup if you haven't put the water in the kettle in the first place.

- As you plan, develop a milestone chart.* This chart identifies the key stages in the project and the deadline/milestone for each of those stages.
- Alongside the critical path and the milestone chart, develop a Gantt chart.* A Gantt chart is a simple bar chart that displays the flow of activities against time. It captures prime information about scheduling.

Keeping your standards high

- Keep the project 'on budget'. Is there someone in the team monitoring this or are you using someone outside the project team?
- Maintain quality standards. While 'quality' is often subjective we usually know it when we see it. What is your gut feeling telling you?

Remember:

- Review progress so far and monitor risk on an ongoing basis.
- You cannot communicate enough.

Stage four – delivering the project

The management approach

- The issue of management style is important. There will be times when a tighter style is needed, where safety, legality and finance are involved, for example. And there will be times when you can be a bit looser. Many people work best when the chains are loosened a little. That said make sure that everyone is aware of where the boundaries are, i.e. not so loose that things take on the characteristics of a free-for-all.
- Make sure you are getting update reports from project team members as you would expect (and have previously agreed).
- Have you developed a planned versus actual schedule?* How up to date is it? Are you where you should be?

Remember:

- Review progress so far and monitor risk on an ongoing basis.
- You cannot communicate enough.

Stage 5 – reviewing the project

- Always review – learn as a project team. Identify what you would do differently next time.
- Did the project deliver what it was meant to?
- Make sure all interested parties get a copy of the project report.

Remember:

- You cannot communicate enough.

---

brilliant recap

- Be clear on the scope of the project – what is the goal?
- Great communication within and beyond the team (with the project sponsor in particular) is essential.
- Failure to plan means project failure.
- Identify the critical activities that must be done to ensure the project moves forward. All project team members must be aware of this 'critical path'.
- Be aware of project risks and reduce the risks where you can.
- Monitor and review regularly as each project stage is delivered.
- Focus the end-of-project review on what you have learned as a team. What would you all do differently next time?
- Feel a bit sad when your successful project team breaks up! Working in a successful project team means strong bonds often develop between team members.

This chapter opened with a few of the challenges presented to Chris Stringer, the Director of the Ancient Human Occupation of Britain project. We leave the last words to him about what can be achieved with a great project team.

On the value of great team working:

That experience (studying the decline of the Neanderthals and the appearance of modern humans) showed me how a team could bring different strengths and knowledge to a project, and achieve something that was much greater than the sum of its individual parts.

On how we can learn from each other:

I've learned so much from the project. The other team members have taught me about a diverse range of subjects, and it's been enlightening to see how people address the same issue from such different perspectives.

On co-opting different areas of expertise:

I hope AHOB will inspire other teams to adopt a multi-disciplinary approach. Our experience shows how much you can achieve this way.

CHAPTER 12

Remote teams

Work has become more cognitively complex, more team-based and collaborative, more dependent on social skills, more time pressured, more reliant on technological competence, more mobile and less dependent on geography.

Don Tapscott and Anthony Williams, 'The Wiki Workplace', taken from their book *Wikinomics*

You could be excused for thinking that the rise and rise of remote working would have killed off the idea of team working but the opposite has proved to be true. Never have brilliant team skills been more important in an environment where you and your colleagues may meet face to face irregularly. E-mail has guaranteed an almost universal form of instant communication but it is used so poorly that often it is a conduit for team communication breakdown rather than an enhancement of team interaction. Four hours a day at the inbox is not healthy.

This chapter explores three kinds of remote team:

1 Teams whose members are regularly away from the 'hub' – these might include field sales teams or where team members work regularly from home.

2 Teams comprising individuals from different organisations or from very diffuse parts of one organisation.

3 In the final section of this chapter 'Net Gen teams' are the focus, often comprising the 'Net Generation' – generally those born after 1977 – who communicate in ways that may only be partially understood by older people. Their 'remoteness' comes not just from geography but also from the way they work. They are included purely to signpost what the future of team working may look like – at least in some organisations. What seems to be true, however, is that the team working 'rules' in the future will not be so different from the 'rules' of the past.

Away from 'the hub'

It is often said that one hour of work at home (or at least away from the office) can take up to three hours of office time to complete. So in one sense working away from the office can mean high achievement. On the other hand, it is easy to forget that fellow team members and other colleagues may not be working at the same pace as you because their circumstances do not allow them

> working away from the office can mean high achievement

to. Firing off 15 e-mails in an hour because you can does not guarantee 15 post-haste responses!

The example below raises several key issues around remote working.

brilliant example

A story – connecting with the hub

Anthony Jay wrote in Management and Machiavelli *of the Roman Empire and the need for all those working in Empire outposts to be totally immersed in the ways of 'Empire' before they left because once gone there would be little communication with Rome. For two thousand years this approach continued to be used in hierarchical 'command and control structures'.*

While these structures started to unravel in the 1970s it is only in the past 10 years that a real quantum leap has been made.

We have the telephone, e-mail, peer-to-peer networking and video conferencing to avoid the need for such extreme indoctrination but nonetheless the lesson about understanding the goals, values and agreed methods of communication between you and 'the hub' remains the same. The onus is on management to communicate with the team – but equally the onus is also on team members to be proactive in keeping in touch and to be clear on what they should be doing.

Sourced from Charles Handy (1993) *Understanding Organisations*, Penguin

What to do when the hub is elsewhere

The goal

Be absolutely clear about what the goals of the team are. You will need to be proactive to keep in touch – don't just rely on others to tell you. Slipping into your own world may bring its personal rewards but won't help the team.

Your role and the goal

As well as the goal be clear on your role in delivering it. As a remote worker you may have a fair degree of freedom to deliver in the way you see best, which is probably why you decided to work in this environment anyway. But be sure that your unique approach is delivering in the result areas.

Acknowledge the trust you have been shown. You are working in a degree of isolation because you are self-motivated, but also because others have faith in you.

World-class communication

Remote team workers may well closely identify with this one – communication – as the key problem, as it is with any kind of team where people are removed from the hub. Here are some pointers to help you access others and be accessible yourself.

✕ brilliant dos and don'ts

Do

✔ Make sure the person delegated with the responsibility for team co-ordination knows your whereabouts. Keep in touch with 'the hub'. Keep 'the hub' interested in – and maybe even excited about – the work you are doing.

✔ Keep the dates when the team has planned to meet face to face as sacrosanct.

✔ See your team as a kind of virtual network – a kind of spider's web – where team members have instant and easy connectivity. Do show a little empathy here however. Not all of us appreciate a BlackBerry message at 3am or a game of relentless ping-pong messaging.

✔ Use informal messaging systems (social networking, e-mail, Skype/Windows Messenger, etc., texting) as a means of keeping in touch with the rest of the team. These informal messaging systems are excellent ways of getting peer group awareness of challenges and enlisting help in overcoming them. But don't let them take over. Most of us are familiar with the old BlackBerry/CrackBerry syndrome.

✔ Be proactive in keeping the team informed of what you are up to. Don't wait to be asked. In the organisation of the future we will all have personal pages on intranets (and some of you may have these already) to keep the team updated with your work, progress, whereabouts, etc. If you do have these already keep them up to date.

✔ Keep up to date with the subtleties and nuances of office life.

✔ Share success stories quickly. A diffuse team needs to keep its morale up.

Don't

✘ Assume that you will always be understood. Many of us are not actually that good at expressing what we mean to say in written form. For you this means always asking how e-mails that you send are likely to be interpreted by others in the team.
It also works the other way. Ask 'Am I reading this right?' when you receive something that is ambiguous and open to different interpretations. Seek clarification if you are unsure.

✘ Let conflict fester – early resolution is essential if the conflict is not to take on a disproportionate life of its own. Conflicts and disagreements can be harder to resolve when you are unable to resolve them face to face.

✘ Be anti-social. Try, however inconvenient, to be available for team social events. They enable you to create and preserve a team bond and keep in touch with what's going on.

brilliant tip

Teams whose members need to communicate as a team on a regular basis, but who rarely physically meet, will need to have regular conference calls. Vary the times when you and your colleagues have these calls – it may be the same people who are having to put in an 'out of hours' stint or who are having to adapt their working day to accommodate the call. 'Spread the inconvenience' in this essential activity. Be prepared to shoulder some of that inconvenience yourself.

Links in the chain

Twenty-five years ago organisations tried to keep much of what they did 'in-house'. Since that time they have tried to take anything out that could just as easily be outsourced: services that can be called on as and when needed rather than kept on the payroll. It means that many people find themselves part of a

many people find themselves part of a wider team

wider team beyond their own organisation. The team might comprise suppliers, consultants, technicians, advertising people, PR, even van drivers and so on. This section assumes that you are in some kind of co-ordination role.

Some of the challenges might include the following.

Differing priorities

Everyone having their own priorities for their part of the project – which aren't necessarily the priorities of the task in hand – so the team requires constant management/realignment. This makes your job a constant juggling act.

Communication methods

Where yours or others' favoured method of communication is not used by some parts of the team. Plenty of people have e-mail and then don't check it for three days.

Priority

What is a big piece of work for you (and therefore priority) might actually be very small (and therefore less of a priority) for other team members.

Positive actions you can take

Overall

Although you might not be leading the team *per se* that should not prevent you from 'taking the lead'. You role here is to:

- maintain good relationships that work even in difficult times; and

- keep everyone conscientious about their part of the task – and deliver on time and on budget.

Communication

Your role here is to:

- ensure communications have been received and understood;

- be aware of each team member's preferred method of communication – the one they respond quickest to (that might mean you use e-mail, fax, verbal or modern web-based networking platforms to get one simple message out to the various links in the team chain); and

- check that communications have been received and understood – ask for confirmation of receipt, never assume.

What unites us?

Identify and use as a motivational tool the shared incentives that exist between all team members. These might include the following:

- If this 'project' or piece of work is for client use there is the possibility of repeat business if you all keep your particular client in the chain happy and/or the overall client happy.

- The continuing freedom to work more flexibly to your own agenda rather than to a corporate dictate.

Clearly some of these actions will relate specifically to your work but do work hard to identify the unifying factors. Make them work for you when you need them.

Something to think about – the way of the future?

▶ brilliant example

In their seminal book *Wikinomics* authors Don Tapscott and Anthony Williams talk about 'Wiki Workplaces' and chronicle the antics of 'The Geek Squad' – part of the massive 'Best Buy' corporation in the US. Here teams of service engineers play 'Battlefield 2' (I presume mostly 'boys') but while they fight across virtual battlefields they talk 'shop' over the internet swapping tips, solving technical problems, talking about budgets, etc. Many of the senior managers were completely unaware of this. Fortunately they were open enough to see that the great results meant this entirely inconceivable-to-them method of team collaboration and communication was working. These are teams who have developed methods of peer group communication, problem solving and innovation – usually through technological advancements – that many readers may only partially understand.

The authors demonstrate that team members and co-workers from this 'Net Generation' are collaborating through the use of peer-to-peer networks, wikis, chatrooms, blogs and personal broadcasting and are not just those who operate in what is often disparagingly called 'Geekworld'.

Teams in the twenty-first century are going to be very different:

- They will have methods of communication that may not be completely understood by more senior levels of management.
- They may be brought together on the spur of the moment to problem solve, satisfy an immediate customer requirement or share important information. Many are recognising that in order to respond quickly to market demands recourse to hierarchy is a non-starter.
- They have a far more brutal attitude to working than previous generations. Previous generations favoured time at the office and loyalty as symbols of success. New generations favour task rather than time. *Let's get the job done and move on to something else, or go off and play* is the new mantra.

- Their methods of communication will be self-generating rather than imposed.

- They may communicate by 'broadcasting' themselves to their colleagues. People will say 'This is who I am, this is what I am doing, these are the problems I have got at work, come and talk to me' through peer-to-peer networking and other, as yet unforeseen, methods. And of course they will go and 'talk' to others in the team and beyond in this way.

People always did need to be proactive communicators. In the teams of the future we will all tap into each other's worlds through different kinds of 'virtual' – though no less real – networks. Our interactions will be just as meaningful as before: they will just be different.

people always did need to be proactive communicators

What will not be different, however, are all of those wonderful things in this book that brilliant teams have done for thousands of years and will do for thousands of years more.

brilliant recap

- Don't lose sight of core objectives – yours and the team's.

- Communication, unsurprisingly, is the key here – use proactive and innovative approaches to stay in touch.

- Bear in mind that the way you like to communicate may not be the way that others like to do so.

- Be available and responsive to requests.

- Recognise the common interest that exists between you and other team members.

- And finally, be open to different ways of doing things. As long as they are ethical and they work – who are you to criticise?

This chapter has given a flavour of what teams will increasingly look like in the future. What is interesting is that many of the lessons in this book about great team working – clear goals, awareness of the role you perform, strong relationships, etc. – apply equally to the teams of the past and the teams of the future. The methods may be different but the principles remain the same. What is true is that in the future the need for these core principles will be accentuated. If you can keep true to these key principles and marry those with the greater freedom and autonomy that these new teams bring then team working can be as fun and personally rewarding as it always has been.

Conclusion

In one of the most well-known observations on teams ever published Bruce Tuckman, educational psychologist, identified four stages in team development – forming, storming, norming and performing. The four stages can be summarised as follows:

- *Forming*: Where a degree of caution is mixed with excitement as teams establish their purpose, their boundaries and their bonds. Teams in this phase do not usually achieve much.
- *Storming*: The most challenging stage for the team as team members have their own ideas and thoughts about how to progress. A degree of tension may kick in and the team might realise that its goals are not quite as simple as first imagined.
- *Norming*: The ideas of co-operation, collaboration, consultation and constructive discussion take the team forward in a calmer team climate. Spoken or unspoken 'ground rules' are established.
- *Performing*: The team maximises its productivity.

You may recognise these stages in different teams that you have been part of.

These four stages have been added to, with stage five being *adjourning* – where your team takes a step back from performing and reviewing and learns from what it has done.

Mourning

The final stage – stage 6 – is *mourning*, or at least it should be. And this is the real test. If your team has achieved what it set out to do, if you have grown and developed as individuals and as a team, if you have thrived in the company of your team mates (even if you didn't like some of them!) and if you have achieved more than you ever could alone, then the break-up of the team will be touched with a bit of sadness for you and your team mates.

> the break up of the team will be touched with sadness

Those bonds you have developed can be difficult to break. For many people the social environment of 'the team' is a key reason to go to work. But it is time to move on with a degree of personal pride that you were part of something that worked and where you did everything you personally could to make it work. Time to move on armed with the knowledge, skills and confidence that you know what it takes to bring a group of people together into a team and the part you can personally play in doing that whether you are the team's leader or a team member.

Time to move on to your next 'brilliant team'.

References and acknowledgements

I sourced material from the following places. Several of these references have been used in multiple chapters. Rather than repeat references I have highlighted the chapter where the reference source has had its strongest influence.

Chapter 1: It starts with YOU

The energy investment model is being regularly updated, most notably by Ian Taylor, the founder of The Deva Partnership. It features in a book co-authored by him and Karen Jackson entitled *The Power of Difference* (Management Books 2000), and the model is now known by them as 'Roles People Play'. Research indicates that the originator of this model is a combination of the late Claude Lineberry, Don Tosti and Calvin Germain at British Airways and General Motors, although there seems to be some uncertainty about its true origin. I have further adapted the model.

I would like to thank Howard Goldsmith at ICI Dulux for suggesting the idea of sub-dividing the quadrants in the energy investment model. Also, thank you to John Henderson and Barry Webster at ICI Dulux for catalysing the '100 club' idea.

Csikszentmihalyi, Mihaly (1991) *Flow: The Psychology of Optimal Experience*, Harper Perennial (the originator of the idea of the 'flow' state).

Pepper, Art and Laurie (2000) *Straight Life*, Mojo Books (for the Shelley Manne quote and other musical 'team-related' observations).

Chapter 2: You and your team relationships

Goleman, Daniel (1996) *Emotional Intelligence*, Bloomsbury.

Goleman, Daniel (1999) *Working with Emotional Intelligence*, Bloomsbury.

Miller, Douglas (2007) *Don't Worry: How To Beat The Seven Anxieties of Life*, Prentice Hall (see chapter on 'Relationships').

Revans, Reg (1998) *ABC of Action Learning*, Lemos and Crane.

Smith, M. K. (2002) 'Howard Gardner and multiple intelligences', *The Encyclopedia of Informal Education*, www.infed.org/ thinkers/gardner.htm.

Some elements of the section on 'Feedback' came from The Hay Group and a BBC Learning package I worked on with them: 'Beyond Appraisal'.

Chapter 3: What's in a brilliant team?

Armstrong, Lance and Jenkins, Sally (2001) *It's Not About The Bike*, Yellow Jacket Press.

Katzenbach, John and Smith, Douglas (1993) 'The Discipline of Teams', *Harvard Business Review*, March.

For team roles reference Peter Honey's website – www.peter honey.com. I originally 'discovered' these roles in a training video 'Teams and Leaders', available at www.videoarts.co.uk.

Chapter 4: Teams and leadership

Goleman, Daniel, Boyatzis, Richard and McKee, Annie (2002) *The New Leaders*, Time Warner Paperbacks.

John Buchanan, Australian cricket coach is at www.buchanan coaching.com.

Chapter 5: Setting team goals

Brown, Mark (1993) *The Dinosaur Strain*, ICE Books.

Covey, Steven (1989) *The Seven Habits of Highly Effective People*, Simon and Schuster.

Kohn, Steven and O'Donnell, Vincent (2007) *The Six Habits of Highly Effective Teams*, Career Press.

Miller, Douglas (2005) *Positive Thinking, Positive Action*, BBC Books.

Chapter 6: Team meetings and briefings

Parts of this chapter were sourced from the writings over the years of training consultant, writer and old friend Pat Mitchell – www.patmitch.demon.co.uk.

Chapter 7: Teams and decision making

Rickards, Tudor (1988) *Creativity and Problem Solving at Work*, Gower.

Chapter 8: Teams under pressure

Pink, Daniel H (2008) *A Whole New Mind*, Marshall Cavendish.

Warren, Eve and Toll, Caroline (1997) *The Stress Workbook*, Nicholas Brealey Publishing.

Chapter 9: The 10 classic team traps

Anacona, Deborah (2007) 'Teams That Lead, Innovate and Succeed', HBR Ideacast, August.

Levy, Paul (2001) 'The Nut Island Effect, When Good Teams Go Wrong', *Harvard Business Review*, March.

http//:uk.youtube.com/watch?v=sFBOQzSk14c (for the Monty Python piece).

Chapter 10: Creative and problem-solving teams

Coyne, Kevin, Clifford, Patricia and Dye, Renee (2007) 'Breakthrough Thinking From Inside the Box', *Harvard Business Review*, December.

Miller, Douglas (2007) *Brilliant Idea*, Prentice Hall.

Access www.slate.com/id/2183058/?from=rss for an online article by Larry Brilliant – 'How Google decided what to give to'.

The phrase 'idea piggy-backing' was given to me by Mark Brown.

Chapter 11: Project teams

Barker, Stephen and Cole, Rob (2007) *Brilliant Project Management*, Prentice Hall.

Stringer, Chris (2006) *Homo Britannicus*, Allen Lane (the appendix has some great observations about project teams).

I would like to acknowledge the help of Nigel Roberts in the preparation of this chapter.

Chapter 12: Remote teams

Tapscott, Don and Williams, Anthony (2007) *Wikinomics: How Mass Collaboration Changes Everything*, Atlantic Books.

Debbie Mules at interiors-ART, an international art consultancy, provided valuable first-hand insights into self-organising teams and her own in particular.

Also by the author

Positive Thinking, Positive Action (2005) BBC Active

The Positive Mental Attitude Pocketbook (2005) Management Pocketbooks

Make Your Own Good Fortune: How to Seize Life's Opportunities (2006) BBC Active

Don't Worry: How to Beat the Seven Anxieties of Life (2007) Prentice Hall

Brilliant Idea (2007) Prentice Hall

The Nurturing Innovation Pocketbook (2009) Management Pocketbooks

the brilliant series

Fast and engaging, the *Brilliant* series works hard to make sure you stand out from the crowd. Each *Brilliant* book has been carefully crafted to ensure everything you read is practical and applicable – to help you make a difference now.

9780273722328 — brilliant Project Management — *What the best project managers know, do and say* — Stephen Barker and Rob Cole

9780273720591 — brilliant Leader — *What the best leaders know, do and say* — Simon Cooper

9780273717355 — brilliant Coaching — *How to be a brilliant coach in your workplace* — Julie Starr

9780273743217 — brilliant Networking — *What the best networkers know, do and say*

9780273726463 — brilliant Selling — *What the best salespeople know, do and say* — Jeremy Cassell and Tom Bird

9780273725114 — brilliant Pitch — *What to know, do and say to make the perfect pitch* — Shaun Vergi

9780273721239 — brilliant Marketing — *What the best marketers know, do and say* — Richard Hall

9780273712350 — brilliant Negotiations — *What the best negotiators know, do and say* — Nic Peeling

9780273734147 — brilliant Decision Making — *Take control of your career, relationships, health and happiness* — Robbie Steinhouse

9780273714804 — brilliant IDEA — Douglas Miller

9780273730675 — brilliant Presentation — *What the best presenters know, do and say* — Richard Hall — Revised 2nd Edition

9780273730910 — brilliant Budgets and Forecasts — *Your practical guide to preparing and presenting financial information* — Malcolm Secrett